31 Days to Survival

A Complete Plan for Emergency Preparedness

Get a medical kit.

Get your spouse onboard.

Buy basic survival supplies.

16 Build a box trap.

17 Get a dental checkup.

18 Make a water filter.

...t and stress.

23 Plan your survival garden.

24 Take a trip to the gunshop.

25 Make surviv... kit for automobile.

30 Find like-minded friends.

31 Learn to tie a knot.

M.D. Creekmore

Paladin Press • Boulder, Colorado

Also by M.D. Creekmore
Dirt-Cheap Survival Retreat

31 Days to Survival:
A Complete Plan for Emergency Preparedness
by M.D. Creekmore
Copyright © 2012 by M.D. Creekmore

ISBN 13: 978-1-61004-648-0
Printed in the United States of America

Published by Paladin Press, a division of
Paladin Enterprises, Inc.
Gunbarrel Tech Center
7077 Winchester Circle
Boulder, Colorado 80301 USA, +1.303.443.7250

Direct inquiries and/or orders to the above address.

PALADIN, PALADIN PRESS, and the "horse head" design
are trademarks belonging to Paladin Enterprises and
registered in United States Patent and Trademark Office.

All rights reserved. Except for use in a review, no
portion of this book may be reproduced, stored in or
introduced into a retrieval system, or transmitted in any
form without the express written permission of the publisher.
The scanning, uploading, and distribution of this book by the
Internet or any other means without the permission of the
publisher is illegal and punishable by law. Please respect the
author's rights and do not participate in any form of electronic
piracy of copyrighted material.

Neither the author nor the publisher assumes
any responsibility for the use or misuse of
information contained in this book.

Visit our website at www.paladin-press.com

Saginaw Chippewa Tribal College
2274 Enterprise Drive
Mt. Pleasant, MI 48858

WITHDRAWN

Welcome. Who among us doesn't want to survive? We're born with the desire to survive, but unfortunately many in our increasingly dependent society look to others for relief and assistance following a disaster. The fact is that help from government, family, or neighbors is often unavailable when needed most, and in the end you may have only yourself to count on. Will you be ready? Do you know what to do and how to do it? Have you made plans and stored the necessary supplies and gear to see you through a long-term disaster?

If not, *31 Days to Survival* will help you prepare to survive both short- and long-term disasters. You just have to make up your mind and get started. Anyone can do it; all you have to do is follow the step-by-step advice in this book. I can assure you that my plan is not difficult—I've made every step as clear and easy to follow as possible.

Each day in the 31-day project outlines a specific task for you to do. This approach is designed so that you come away from each day's assignment having not only read about how to do it (or how someone else has done it), but having actually completed a survival task yourself using the knowledge presented for that day, thus increasing your survival skills and your readiness to survive a long-term disaster.

Don't be intimidated by the "31 day" schedule. You can take as much time as is necessary to complete each assignment.

Indeed, for most readers some tasks will certainly take longer than one day to complete. Some could require a month or more, depending on each individual's abilities, schedules, and resources. Complete each assignment at your own pace. The most important thing is to persevere with each assignment; before you know it, you will have accomplished your goal of being prepared to survive a long-term disaster. Trust me—it is a great feeling.

Because you can proceed at your own pace and in your own way, *31 Days to Survival* will work for anyone. It is the most versatile and helpful resource in the crowded survival field.

By the end of the 31 days you will have:

✔ Built a rotating canned-food shelf and filled your pantry with nutritious, durable food

✔ Accumulated the right firearms for both foraging and defense

✔ Assembled both first aid and dental kits

✔ Constructed a homemade water filter

✔ Put together a functional 72-hour and an every-day carry (EDC) kit

✔ Learned firearms safety and first aid techniques

✔ Made and used traps for small game and fish

✔ Collected tools for your survival garden

✔ Acquired a survival tool kit

✔ Found like-minded friends

✔ Learned to tie a knot

✔ And much more . . .

Are you ready? Let's get started . . .

Check your skills.

Any person who sets out to acquire a set of survival skills must start with a brutally honest self-assessment. If you don't make a truthful appraisal of where you are in terms of your survival skills and knowledge, you have no reliable means of getting to where you want to be.

Do an inventory. In what areas are you most skilled? Where are you definitely lacking? Are you well versed in firearms but lack knowledge about water purification? Have you amassed an impressive food pantry but have no way to protect that food should the need arise? Do you have an excellent first aid kit but don't know how to use it?

Just as a business that fails to take regular inventory cannot succeed, neither can a survivor who doesn't tabulate his resources. You need a starting point, and today's assignment is to take an inventory of your essential survival skills.

As you read though the following list, check off those skills you have mastered so you can focus on those skills on which you need to improve.

1. *Food processing.* Many survival planners overlook food processing in favor of more exciting elements of preparedness. This is a mistake. Learning how to prepare basic survival foods is one of the most important elements of long-term disaster preparedness.

2. *Bulk food storage.* Without adequate quantities of stored foods, your demise is virtually guaranteed after a major catastrophe. Storing and rotating basic grains, beans, and other foodstuffs isn't difficult; anyone can learn how to do it properly in an hour or two. You will find everything you need to know within the pages of this book.

3. *Emergency medical care.* Every survivalist should have sufficient medical training. A good start is taking a basic cardiopulmonary resuscitation (CPR) and first aid class; check with your local Red Cross for scheduling. If time and finances allow, taking EMT classes is an excellent idea. Don't overlook herbal medicine, which may be all you will have to work with after a disaster.

4. *Gardening.* Because of space and finances, most of us cannot cache enough food to last the rest of our lives. We'll need to replace our stored foods with fresh supplies. Gardening is an excellent way to do this and can be easily learned with instruction and practice. It is amazing the amount of food that can be grown in a small space under proper conditions.

5. *Preserving food.* Food preservation is an important survival skill, as most fresh foods spoil fairly quickly, resulting in a loss of quality, edibility, and nutritional value. You should learn to can, dry, freeze, cure (salt or sugar), smoke, pickle, bury, vacuum-pack, jelly, and/or pot food.

6. *Hunting.* Contrary to popular belief, all wild game will *not* disappear after a collapse, natural or manmade. Most people would rather stand in a food line waiting for a handout than scour the backwoods for game. And let's not forget that the extent of most people's hunting skills doesn't go beyond the latest hunting-themed video game.

7. *Trapping.* Trapping is more practical under survival conditions than hunting. By setting a trap, you can be

other places doing other things while the trap does the hunting for you. Learn to build and set snares, deadfalls, box traps, fish traps, and steel traps. Becoming a proficient trapper is not difficult—all you need to do is get off the couch and learn by doing.

8. *Firearms repair.* Basic firearms repair (replacement of broken parts) isn't difficult if you have the parts needed when something breaks. You don't need to learn how to repair every make and model of firearm in existence. You do need to have an in-depth understanding of *your* firearms: how they work and how to maintain and repair them.

9. *Self-defense skills.* The most effective self-defense techniques are also the easiest to master. Striking vulnerable points, biting, and eye gouging are simple and effective techniques that can be learned quickly and, when applied with aggression and precision, can bring down the most determined attacker.

10. *Firearms proficiency.* If you're new to firearms, a basic safety course is highly recommended before learning defensive skills. Concealed-carry permit classes are held in most areas, as are hunter education programs. I suggest you participate in both. The National Rifle Association (NRA) offers a number of classes that are most helpful.

11. *Water purification.* Another simple skill often overlooked is water acquisition and purification.

12. *Using tools.* You should have a survival toolbox of basic tools, including hammers, saws, drills, screwdrivers, winches, vise grips, wire cutters, and files. Your toolbox should also include the skills needed to put these tools to good use.

13. *Raising small livestock.* Raising livestock for food goes hand-in-hand with gardening, hunting, and trapping to ensure sustenance during hard times. I highly recommend *Barnyard in Your Backyard* by Gail Damerow, which covers everything you need

to know about making livestock part of your survival food plan.

14. *Home power.* While it may be possible to survive with no electrical power at all, having some source of electrical current will make life much easier. My solar setup cost me under $600, including the batteries, and the price of building my homemade electrical generator amounted to just under $100.

15. *Investing.* After getting your survival necessities in order (e.g., food, water, medical supplies, shelter, defense), you need to start thinking about investing in barter goods, such as .22-caliber ammo, pocketknives, and "junk" silver coins. Just be sure not to make the mistake of going into debt while investing in these metals.

✔ *Today's Assignment:*

Check your skills (be honest!) against the list above. If there are areas in which you are lacking (and there will be if you're being honest), then get to work filling in the gaps. Most of what you need to know can be found in the following pages.

Start your

preparedness

binder.

What's the most important component of your preparedness preparation? Is it water, food, shelter, emergency
medicine, defense? The correct answer is . . . none of
the above.

Yes, you need those essential life-supporting items, but if
you ask me what the most important part of survival planning is
I would say information. Some will disagree with me on this,
but that's OK. We all have our opinions, and that's great. Just
don't let your beliefs nullify your good judgment and lessen
your chance of survival.

Information and individual survival skills are key to your
survival, and both require a well-rounded and well-organized
survival library. Having a good survival library is, in my opinion, just as important as having a well-stocked pantry. As they
say, knowledge is power; when it comes to survival, you can't
have too much information or knowledge.

But books are expensive, and building a survival library covering all the needed skills can run into hundreds or even thousands of
dollars, which most of us don't have. If you have an extra $2,000 to
purchase books and other related research materials, buy all the
books, periodicals, and videos you can. Unfortunately, most of us
don't have that kind of money. How are you supposed to build a
survival library without taking out an extra mortgage on your
home, selling your bodily fluids or parts, or pimping yourself out
on the street corner?

Well, you can buy used books, and one economical source for used books is online vendors, especially Amazon. This is not to denigrate yard sales, library sales, estate sales, or used book stores, but survival and gun books are rarely found at "sales." At Amazon you can find anything, and the search takes seconds.

Even buying used books may be more than your budget can afford these days, so I have a cheaper option for you: a survival binder or binders. Let's get started . . .

WHAT IS A SURVIVAL BINDER?

A survival binder is simply a book of collected information gathered from various sources both online and offline. You can use any type of binder you want, but I prefer the cheapest three-ring one I can find that is sturdy enough to be handled or transported.

Most office supply stores carry 20-pound, 8.5 x 11-inch, three-hole-punched paper for use in this type of binder. If you can't find the paper with the holes in stock, a three-hole paper punch works well. That's what I use so I can add pages taken from magazines, newspapers, letters, or books to the binder, and not just items I have copied onto the punched paper.

You might consider waterproof paper. There are a number of suppliers of various grades; simply Google "waterproof paper." A poor-man's alternative is to haunt new house construction sites for scraps of Tyvec "house wrap." It's printable, waterproof, durable, punchable, and usually free in scraps, and it cuts with scissors. Of course, waterproof paper doesn't do much good if the ink is not also waterproof. Some copy/printer inks are waterproof; some are not. So use the good stuff to print downloads you want to keep through hell and high water. For your own note-taking, the Sharpie waterproof marker is durable. Some ballpoint ink is waterproof; some is not. Water-based inks often do not go on, and pencil usually rubs off.

Another option is using clear plastic three-ring envelopes (the soft ones, not the stiff glassine ones). They come in all sorts of configurations, including ones with half-pockets for clippings and ones that zip-lock watertight. They also make a heavy-duty version as used in factories for holding work orders that is also oil resistant and comes three-ring punched.

To make it easier to access information in your binders, you should label each with the subjects covered. If you don't do this from the beginning, as your library grows you'll have to spend a lot of time flipping through each binder to find the one with the information you need. I write the subject on a 1-inch-wide by 8-inch-long strip of paper and tape it to the spine with clear 2-inch packaging tape encasing the label. If your writing isn't legible, you can type the labels or use a label-maker (a good one runs about $12). Index tabs make retrieval quicker if you have individual "chapters" in your binders.

One of the great things about the survival binder system is that—unlike many survival books out there covering a broad range of subjects, with only one or two being relevant to you—your binder includes only those subjects that you need, saving you time, space, and money. Plus, the binders take less storage space and are more portable than books or video cases.

What you put in your survival binder will depend on several factors, including but not limited to your location, survival plans, and skill level. For example, if you retreat to an area where raising a garden isn't feasible, then adding information on gardening wouldn't make a lot of sense. Or if you live on the Cumberland Plateau of Tennessee, then you won't have a binder devoted to desert survival skills. You get the idea. Don't waste time or resources on things you won't use.

Now where to find reliable, printable information for free? (I love that word . . . FREE.) Well, blogs are one great source. For example, my blog (www.the survivalistblog.net) is a treasure trove of information on a wide variety of survival topics from knowledgeable sources, and the articles are all free for the taking. Check out the print-friendly button at the bottom of each post.

Where else can you find free material? A good place to start when looking for information on gardening, livestock, and homesteading is cooperative extension publications from county, state, and federal agencies, such as the U.S. Department of Agriculture. Here is the URL for my state extension office:

https://utextension.tennessee.edu/Pages/default.aspx. Your state will have a similar agency, as will most counties. Go online and Google "state extension office" or "county extension office." Most of the publications are free or reasonably priced.

The Federal Emergency Management Agency (FEMA) and the American Red Cross have a wealth of free information on emergency preparedness and survival on their respective sites ready to download and print. A great place to start your preparations is FEMA's *Are You Ready?,* which is available at www.ready.gov/are-you-ready-guide.

Your state's department of natural resources web page is a terrific place to find advice on such topics as trapping, butchering game, hunting, vegetation, and other relevant topics.

If you're looking for military tactics, sites abound that allow you to download and print manuals detailing everything from outdoor survival and weapons training to demolitions.

Another good link is http://publications.usa.gov/USAPubs.php. This federal government site provides a lot of publications for free or at minimal cost, although you may have to weed through a lot of garbage to find what you need.

A quick and useful way to find printable information on any subject is to do a Google search for the topic with PDF (portable document format) added to the search term: for example, "raising tomatoes PDF." PDF files are great because they are easy to print and put into your binder.

If you want to be more selective about what you include in your binder, you can highlight the information of interest, cut and paste it to a Word file, and then print that out and add it to your binder. This way, you have only what you want.

Today's Assignment:

Take a close look at your survival plans and skills, and write down those areas where you need more information. Then start a survival binder system with the correct information to fill in the gaps.

DAY	*Find storage space*
3	*and build a rotating*
	canned-food shelf.

I f you live in an apartment, mobile home, travel trailer, or other small space, you may be wondering where in the heck you're going to put all the food and survival gear recommended in the following days' assignments.

Well to be honest, you may not have enough storage space for everything, but you probably have more available space than you think. Here are a few ideas to help you find the necessary space to get your food storage squared away after your shopping trip on day nine.

This is an example of what you *don't* want your food storage to look like. Disorganized shelves make it difficult to manage and rotate food properly.

1. *Under the bed.* Flat rollout bins for under-bed storage work great. Also consider putting risers (such as concrete blocks) under your bed so you can fit more things underneath.
2. *In the bedroom closet.* Be sure to add a lock to the door to keep anyone from looking inside.
3. *Under a staircase.* The space under staircases can be enclosed and perhaps made into hidden storage rooms.
4. *Under or inside a coffee table.* With some types of tables, the contents can be completely hidden from view.
5. *In the laundry room.* Adding shelves or cabinets in the laundry room can provide storage for certain types of foodstuffs. But be aware that heat and moisture could be a problem and may shorten the shelf life of certain foods. Do your research and see what items can safely be stored in this environment.
6. *In the attic.* Again, heat or cold may be a problem here and could limit shelf life of certain foods. Be selective about what you store here.
7. *Under the floor.* If you have a large crawl space, you may be able to partition a storage area here. You could even build a secret door through the floor into the storage area. You also have to be careful what type of foodstuffs you store here, factoring in exposure to heat and cold and rodent-proofing your stash.
8. *Between wall studs.* Add cabinets or shallow shelves between the studs along inside walls. You could easily retrofit a removable panel that is backed by magnets to hold it in place for a secret storage area. Just be sure the panel material matches the rest of the wall.
9. *Floor-to-ceiling wall space.* When building shelves or cabinets, utilize all the space from floor to ceiling. Many people ignore valuable overhead or lower storage space because it isn't as easy to access.
10. *Inside furniture.* Buy furniture with built-in storage space. Examples include coffee and occasional tables,

ottomans, storage cubes, and trunks, which do double-duty as tables or seating areas.

11. And the most important tip of all: declutter your home and storage area. This increases your storage capacity and makes retrieval faster and easier.

For storage of canned goods, consider buying or building a rotating shelving system. This type of shelving unit does the work of turning and rotating the cans for you automatically, thus extending shelf life by ensuring that the oldest cans in your shelf are used first. Shelfreliance.com sells ready-made units, or you can build your own to fit your needs by going to www.wiki-how.com/Build-a-Rotating-Canned-Food-Shelf and following the step-by-step instructions.

When building a rotating canned-food shelf, you don't need to get fancy with the woodwork (unless you want to) or follow the directions given on the site too rigidly. For example, the measurements given can be modified to meet your space limitations or storage requirements.

Today's Assignment:

Find and prepare space in your home/retreat to store your survival food and gear. In the coming days, you'll be going shopping, and you'll need a place to store all those items.

DAY	*Make a list of what*
4	*and how much your*
	family eats in a week.

rint the worksheet on page 16 and write down everything
you and your family eat for each day in the corresponding
blocks. By doing this simple exercise, you'll get a much better
idea of what and how much food you'll need over a given period
than you could from any other list or online storage calculator.

FOOD-STORAGE SHELF LIFE

Print a copy of the food-storage shelf life chart on page 17 and
post it in your storage area. Listing specific foods and their shelf
life is nothing more than an educated guess, as there are too many
variables involved, such as altitude, age and condition of food
when it was bought, and the storage conditions in your pantry.

Generally speaking, most foods remain edible past the listed
expiration date, but they may lose some or most of their nutritional value. If the food looks and smells normal past the listed
use-by date, then it is probably still safe to eat . . . but then again,
maybe not. Check the FDA site www.fda.gov/Food/ScienceRe-
search/LaboratoryMethods/BacteriologicalAnalyticalManual-
BAM/ucm109398.htm for a wealth of information on determining
the safety of canned foods. I toss out cans that are swollen or
rusted around the seams, but in the end you'll have to use your
own judgment. Remember, the listings in the chart on page 17 are
only suggested shelf life times; they are not guaranteed.

DAILY FOOD CHART

Monday: _____

_____

_____

_____

Tuesday: _____

_____

_____

_____

Wednesday: _____

_____

_____

_____

Thursday: _____

_____

_____

_____

Friday: _____

_____

_____

_____

Saturday: _____

_____

_____

_____

Sunday: _____

_____

_____

_____

Notes: _____

_____

_____

_____

_____

_____

FOOD-STORAGE SHELF LIFE

Food Type	Estimated Shelf Life
Baking powder	18–24 months
Baking soda	2 years
Beans, dried (e.g., black, lima, pinto, navy)	1–5 years
Bouillon products	1 year
Cake mixes	6–9 months
Canned foods	1–5 years or more
Chili powder	6–12 months
Cocoa mixes	8–12 months
Coffee, canned	2 years, unopened
Coffee, vacuum-packed	8–12 months
Corn, dried in kernel form	Indefinitely; viable as seed for generations
Corn syrup	3–5 years
Cornmeal	Dry and unopened, up to 5 years
Crackers	3 months
Dry soup mix	1–2 years
Flour, enriched white	Dry and unopened, up to 5 years
Fruit drink mix, powdered	1–2 years
Gelatin, flavored (e.g., Jell-O)	6–12 months
Honey	Indefinitely
Jams and jellies	1–3 years
Legumes	1 year (10 years or more if properly stored)
Lentils	1–4 years
Mayonnaise	2–3 months
Molasses	2–3 years
Milk, evaporated	6–12 months
Milk, nonfat dried	2–5 years (store in a cool place)
Oats, rolled	Dry and unopened, up to 8 years
Pasta, dried	2 years or more
Peanut butter	1–3 years
Pectin	1 year
Popcorn	1–2 years
Rice, white	Indefinitely
Salad dressings, bottled	1 year
Salt, iodized	Indefinitely
Sauce and gravy mixes	6 months
Shortening	3 months
Soybeans	1–5 years
Spices	1–3 years
Sugar, brown	4–6 months
Sugar, white	Indefinitely
Tea bags	18 months
Tea, instant	2 years
Vanilla extract	1 year
Vegetable oil	6–12 months
Vinegar	2–3 years
Vitamin and mineral supplements	1–3 years
Whole wheat	Indefinitely
Yeast	Pkg. exp. date

MAKE A LIST OF WHAT YOUR FAMILY EATS

Build a solar cooker.

I f you live in an area that receives a lot of sunlight throughout the year, solar cooking can be a great way to use this resource. Solar cooking is a simple, safe, convenient, and infinitely renewable way to cook food without depleting your liquid fuel storage or alerting anyone to your location, as you would if cooking over a fire or on top of a wood stove.

If you live in the southwestern desert areas, solar may be your best and only easily renewable energy source for cooking

This simple solar cooker can be built with nothing more than a cardboard box, aluminum foil, and tape.

and day-to-day energy needs. Walking for miles to collect enough wood to cook isn't an efficient trade-off of time and energy spent versus calories received. Solar cooking uses the least amount of individual energy and makes the most sense from a survivability standpoint, and I suggest you use it to your advantage whenever possible.

You could buy an elaborate (and expensive) reflective-type solar cooker, but I prefer to keep things simple and cheap, using scrounged materials if possible. All you need to build this solar cooker is two or three cardboard boxes (a wooden box is even better), aluminum foil, tape or glue, and a box cutter or sharp knife.

This solar cooker design is nothing more than a box with foil-covered panels set at the appropriate angles to efficiently reflect the sun's rays and heat back to the inside of the box, thus providing heat to cook.

This design is idiot simple, but you could improve the concept by building your cooker from such materials as wood and constructing a framed glass and hinged door. There are numerous efficient homemade solar oven designs available in books and online, and I'm sure as you experiment you'll come up with some great improvements of your own. What you do is limited only by your imagination, needs, and time.

CONSTRUCTION

To start, you'll need two or three cardboard boxes: one for the oven itself and the others from which to cut the panels and other needed pieces. The box for the oven itself should be rectangular and taller than the inside width. For example, the box I used for the oven shown in the photos measured 16 inches long, 12 inches wide, and 19 inches high.

The first step is to draw a line approximately 2 inches above the bottom of the box along one of the wider sides and then cut down from the top along each corner seam to that line and carefully fold down the front panel at that point.

From one of the other boxes, cut and fit enough rectangular pieces to build up the bottom of the box to correspond with the

Top view of the solar cooking box showing the proper angles of the cardboard inserts and how they are positioned inside the box.

Side view showing the adjustable front panel and the string used to hold the panel in the desired position.

"hinge" where the front panel folds down. I glued each piece one to the other as I built the bottom of the box up to the desired level, but this is optional.

Next measure and cut two pieces of cardboard from one of the boxes to form two panels set at a 90-degree angle inside the box, as shown in the photo. Now cover and tape, staple, or glue aluminum foil over these two panels as well as to the bottom of the box and the inside of the hinged panel.

Now fit and secure the two inside panels inside the box, as shown in the photo. I used clear tape for this step. You could make the oven more efficient by filling the open spaces behind each of the inside panels with insulation and covering the top of the space with cardboard pieces cut to fit over the top corner spaces. You could also paint the outside of the box with a flat black paint, thus increasing heating efficiency.

When you are cooking something in this oven, set it in the sun and adjust the front panel to an appropriate angle to catch and reflect as much sunlight and heat as possible into the box. As you can see from the photo, I used two screws and a piece of string to adjust and hold the panel at the desired angle. During the cooking process, you need to adjust the box and front panel to correspond with the angle of the sun as it moves.

When looking for cooking pots to use with your solar oven, keep in mind that dark-colored pots made with thin materials work best and that metal pots heat faster than ceramic or earthenware ones. You can order solar cooking pots online from several different sources. If you're going to do a lot of cooking in your oven, these solar pots may be worth looking into because the finish is specifically designed to absorb the light and the heat from the sun instead of reflecting it, as many conventional cooking pots do.

The time it takes for water to reach a desirable cooking temperature depends on season, time of day, altitude, and several other factors. In July and August, I can have hot soup in under an hour, but on cool or cloudy days it can take several hours for the food to even become warm. Solar cooking is not an exact science and is learned mostly by doing.

Using a clear cover on your pots provides two advantages: you get the hothouse effect, and you minimize heat loss due to casual air circulation or, especially, a stiff breeze.

There are a number of great books available with solar cooker designs, recipes, and cooking tips. I haven't read them all, but I can recommend *Solar Cooking* by Harriet Kofalk.

✔ *Today's Assignment:*

Build a solar cooker using a cardboard box and prepare a dish from your food-storage pantry.

Let's go shopping

for your

72-hour kit.

As with any prepping shopping list, you'll need to tailor the suggestions listed below to meet your specific needs, skills, location, budget, and circumstances. No single shopping list can cover the needs of everyone in every situation.

The items below make up what is commonly referred to as a "72-hour kit"—i.e., enough critical supplies to see you through at least three days during an emergency. This is where you should start your overall preparation. In the following days, we'll build and expand your stockpile to the point where you will be prepared for both short-term and long-term disasters (i.e., those lasting six months or more).

Now let's head to your local shopping mall or department store. Here is your shopping list:

1. *Water.* A three-day supply of bottled water—roughly equal to 1 gallon of water per person per day.
2. *Food.* A three-day supply of nonperishable foods ready to eat without cooking and with minimal water is best.
3. *Radio.* A portable, battery-powered AM/FM radio (shortwave bands are a plus) and at least one set of replacement batteries and one replacement bulb if applicable. Also stash a crank-type radio to use if your battery supply becomes depleted.
4. *Flashlight.* Get one or more good-quality flashlights

and at least one set of replacement batteries and bulbs (don't skimp here; get a good-quality light). Add a crank/ shake type flashlight, and consider solar-charge LED area lights, which are available for a few bucks each and give enough light to last almost all night to allow you to get around camp or inside a tent/cabin.

5. *Basic first aid kit.*
6. *Toiletries.* Personal hygiene items for 72 hours, including toilet paper, feminine supplies (if applicable), hand sanitizer and soap, toothbrush and toothpaste, unwaxed dental floss (for flossing as well as sewing and suturing), and whatever else you need.
7. *Matches.* Make sure you have matches and a waterproof container in which to store them.
8. *Lantern.* Battery-powered lantern and at least one set of replacement batteries.
9. *Whistle.* Make it sturdy plastic if you live in a cold climate.
10. *Clothing.* Extra clothing and footwear suitable to the local climate and season. (Most of you will already have what you need in this area.) The operative words here are *warm* and *dry*.
11. *Cookware.* Kitchen accessories and cooking utensils; manual can and bottle openers (the old military P-38 opener is cheap, always works, and takes up no space); disposable plates, bowls, and silverware; napkins/paper towels.
12. *Special needs.* Personal items, such as prescription medications and supplements; eyeglasses; extra contact lenses, solution, and case; hearing aid and batteries, etc.
13. *Baby items.* Infants need formula/food, bottles and nipples, diapers and wipes, diaper cream, blankets, sterilization equipment, baby medicines, pacifiers, toys, and various other essentials.
14. *Sleeping bag or blanket for warmth.* This should be appropriate for the season, location, and climate. A space blanket takes up little room and works wet.

15. *Personal tools.* A multitool, crowbar, hammer, staple gun, adjustable wrench, bungee cords, roll of wire (stovepipe or single-conductor electrical), and heavy-duty work gloves are nice to have.
16. *Water purification.* Water purification tablets, a purifying filter, or a small bottle of unscented liquid household bleach and an eyedropper will work.
17. *Plastic sheeting, duct tape, and utility knife.* These can be used for covering broken windows or sheltering in place.
18. *Sanitation items.* Large heavy-duty plastic bags and a plastic bucket for waste and sanitation uses.
19. *Stove.* A small multi-fuel backpacker's stove is ideal (Coleman makes an excellent one).
20. *Masks.* Dust masks are essential for each person.
21. *Rope.* You need approximately 100 feet of 550-pound para cord or similar rope product.

Along with these purchases, it's a good idea to keep photocopies of credit and identification cards, health and property insurance policies, and other important documents in a waterproof container. You also need an emergency cash stash: I recommend about $100 in small denominations and several rolls of quarters for phone calls. Don't forget photos of family members and pets for identification purposes if you get separated.

You'll need to put together a list of emergency and personal contact phone numbers as well as a complete list of allergies to any drug (especially antibiotics) or food for each person in your group. Finally, it's a good idea to have an extra set of keys to your house and vehicles.

HOW TO PACK AND STORE YOUR 72-HOUR KIT

The 72-hour kit is designed primarily as an at-home kit but can serve as an evacuation kit if needed, so it needs to be stored in an easy-to-transport container. You want to be able to "grab and go" if you are forced to evacuate your home quickly.

I prefer to "double pack." First, I neatly pack everything into duffel bags or backpacks, and then I store these in plastic totes, making it easy to quickly load everything into my car while still having the option of splitting up the gear among group members if forced to evacuate on foot.

Today's Assignment:

Put together your 72-hour survival kit. This kit will provide what you need to survive 95 percent of disasters and is a great starting point for your preparedness journey.

DAY

7

Schedule a CPR and first aid class for you and your family.

For medical training, at a minimum *everyone* in your group should pass a basic CPR/first aid class. Additionally, nursing, home-health care, or paramedic/EMT classes are well worth the time and will take you well beyond the skills taught in a basic first aid class.

Get as much training in this area as possible. You can't know too much, and you can always learn something new. Plus, these skills will come in handy in many nonemergency situations. Start by contacting your local Red Cross office and signing up for the next available class. Be sure to get all the information and schedules for other medical classes or courses being offered.

The second part of today's assignment is to put together your own medical library. To help you get started, here is a short list of books that I have and recommend:

- Auerbach, Paul S. *Medicine for the Outdoors.* Philadelphia, PA: Elsevier/Mosby, 2001.
- Craig, Glen K. *U.S. Army Special Forces Medical Handbook.* Boulder, CO: Paladin Press, 1988.
- Dickson, Murray. *Where There Is No Dentist.* Berkeley, CA: Hesperian Health Guides, 2010.
- Handal, Kathleen A. *The American Red Cross First Aid & Safety Handbook.* New York: Little, Brown, & Company, 1992.

- NATO. *Emergency War Surgery.* Palm Springs, CA: Desert Publications, 1992.
- Porter, Robert S., editor. *The Merck Manual of Diagnosis and Therapy.* West Point, PA: Merck, Sharp, & Dohme Corporation, 2011.
- U.S. Public Health Service. *Ship's Medicine Chest and Medical Aid at Sea.* Amsterdam, the Netherlands: Fredonia Books, 2001.
- Werner, David, Jane Maxwell, and Carol Thuman. *Where There Is No Doctor.* Berkeley, CA: Hesperian Health Guides, 2011.

✔ *Today's Assignment:*

Enroll in some type of medical training course and start assembling your medical library.

DAY 8

Optimize your time for prepping.

Even though time is a limited resource, we still have 24 hours in a day, which is plenty to do what needs to be done. You just have to reevaluate your priorities. No, I'm not suggesting you abandon spending time with your family or anything so drastic. But then again, isn't safeguarding your family the reason you're prepping in the first place?

Some readers may work 10 or more hours a day and sleep another six to eight, leaving only a few hours for other activities, such as family and prepping. So let's find ways to maximize your prepping time and effectiveness without abandoning the ones you love in the process.

Here are six tips to help you make the most of your time:

1. *Stop reading and start doing.* Reading is important, but only to a point. Remember, to actually learn a skill and retain it, you need to put the book down or get away from the computer and do it. If you're reading about gardening, for example, then go dig up your yard and plant a garden. It's hard to beat hands-on experience.

2. *Focus on the tasks that have the highest impact.* Don't sweat the small stuff—instead, concentrate on tasks that have the most impact on meeting your goals. For the survivalist, the goals usually are to build up your

supply of stored foods and survival gear and to learn new skills. If what you're doing isn't furthering this end, stop doing it and reevaluate your plan.

3. *Don't get distracted.* When learning new survival skills, it's easy to become overwhelmed, leading to distraction and lack of progress. I've found the best way to learn needed is to break things down into smaller parts. For example, you might study storing food one month, preparing it the next month, and trapping game the next. The key is to master one area before moving to the next.

4. *Throw away your television.* You're not going to gain many survival insights watching *American Idol* or another rerun of *That '70s Show.* It's amazing how much time we spend in front of a television, and for the most part it's not going to bring you closer to your emergency-preparedness goals.

5. *Maximize your health.* If you're healthy, you'll have more energy to get things done. Eat healthy foods, exercise regularly, and get enough sleep. Getting into shape will improve your productivity and increase your chances of survival under any circumstances.

6. *Kill two birds with one stone.* You should spend time with your family, but if possible make that time serve double-duty. For instance, take your children camping and use the time to teach them survival skills. To increase their skills, Boy/Girl Scouts and other similar programs are worthwhile for getting kids familiar with the outdoors, learning basic first aid, and so forth. If nothing else, get them old copies of the Scout manuals to read—the older the better. Spend the weekend with your spouse learning to prepare basic foods. Take a first aid course as a couple or, even better, as a family. Go shooting. The most important things are to include your family as much as possible and to make it fun, which will make you closer.

Today's Assignment:

Brainstorm ways to maximize your time as a family for prepping and learning needed survival skills.

DAY 9

Let's go shopping for your year's food supply.

Below you'll find three one-year food storage plans. Each one is geared to different budgets and individual needs. Please note that the items and quantities listed are only suggestions, and it is best to tailor the list to your specific needs.

For example, you may not care for split peas and opt to replace them with an equal amount of a comparable food you prefer, such as 10 pounds of pinto or black beans. Doing this will personalize your food storage and help to avoid the waste and shock that can result from a dramatic change in diet.

"I HAVE A FULL-TIME JOB, ONE-PERSON, ONE-YEAR FOOD STORAGE PLAN"

Basics:
❑ Cornmeal, 25 pounds
❑ Flour, 25 pounds
❑ Oats, rolled, 25 pounds
❑ Pasta, 25 pounds
❑ Rice, 50 pounds
❑ Wheat berries, 150 pounds

Fats and Oils:
❑ Mayonnaise, 2 quarts
❑ Peanut butter, 4 pounds

❏ Salad dressing, 1 quart
❏ Shortening, 4 pounds
❏ Vegetable oil, 4 gallons

Legumes:
❏ Dry soup mix, 5 pounds
❏ Lentils, 10 pounds
❏ Lima beans, 5 pounds
❏ Pinto beans, 50 pounds
❏ Soybeans, 10 pounds
❏ Split peas, 10 pounds

Sugars:
❏ Brown sugar, 3 pounds
❏ Corn syrup, 3 pounds
❏ Gelatin (flavored), 1 pound
❏ Honey, 5 pounds
❏ Jams and jellies, 5 pounds
❏ Molasses, 1 pound
❏ Powdered fruit drink mix, 6 pounds
❏ White sugar, 40 pounds

Milk:
❏ Dried milk, 75 pounds
❏ Evaporated milk, 12 pounds

Cooking Essentials:
❏ Baking powder, 1 pound
❏ Baking soda, 1 pound
❏ Salt, iodized, 10 pounds
❏ Vinegar, 3 gallons
❏ Yeast, 0.5 pound

Spices (choose from these based on your tastes and preferences):
❏ Basil
❏ Black pepper
❏ Cayenne pepper

- ❏ Chili powder
- ❏ Cinnamon
- ❏ Garlic salt or powder
- ❏ Marjoram
- ❏ Oregano
- ❏ Rosemary
- ❏ Sage
- ❏ Thyme

Canned Foods:
- ❏ Fruits and vegetables, 25 pounds
- ❏ Meats, 50 pounds

Supplements:
- ❏ Multivitamin and mineral supplement, approximately 365 count
- ❏ Vitamin C 500 mg., 365 count

Water/Beverages:
- ❏ Bleach (unscented), 1 gallon
- ❏ Coffee or tea (optional), based on your drinking habits
- ❏ Water, 14 gallons. (**Note:** If you live in an arid region, you'll need to store considerably more.)

"I HAVE A PART-TIME JOB, ONE-PERSON, ONE-YEAR FOOD-STORAGE PLAN"

Food:
- ❏ Baking powder, 2 pounds
- ❏ Beans (e.g., pinto, black, navy), 100 pounds
- ❏ Dried or canned fruits and vegetables, 100 pounds
- ❏ Dried milk, 50 pounds
- ❏ Feed wheat from your local farmers market, 300 pounds
- ❏ Honey or sugar, 25 pounds
- ❏ Multivitamin, vitamin C (500 mg.), and mineral supplements, approximately 365 count
- ❏ Rice, 100 pounds

- ❏ Salt, iodized, 5 pounds
- ❏ Vegetable oil, 4 gallons
- ❏ Yeast, 1 pound

Water/Beverages:
- ❏ Bleach (unscented), 1 gallon
- ❏ Coffee or tea (optional), based on your drinking habits
- ❏ Water, 14 gallons. (**Note:** If you live in an arid region, you'll need to store considerably more.)

"I DON'T WANT TO MESS WITH WHOLE WHEAT AND HAVE VERY LITTLE MONEY, ONE-PERSON, ONE-YEAR FOOD-STORAGE PLAN"

Food:
- ❏ Baking powder, 2 pounds
- ❏ Beans (e.g., pinto, black, navy), 50 pounds
- ❏ Cornmeal, 25 pounds
- ❏ Dried and canned fruits and vegetables, 100 pounds
- ❏ Dried milk, 50 pounds
- ❏ Flour, 50 pounds
- ❏ Multivitamin, vitamin C (500 mg.), and mineral supplements, approximately 365 count
- ❏ Oats, rolled, 25 pounds
- ❏ Rice, 50 pounds
- ❏ Split peas, 25 pounds
- ❏ Salt, iodized, 5 pounds
- ❏ Sugar, white, 25 pounds
- ❏ Tuna, 50 cans
- ❏ Vegetable oil, 4 gallons
- ❏ Yeast, 0.5 pound

Water/Beverages:
- ❏ Bleach (unscented), 1 gallon
- ❏ Coffee or tea (optional), based on your drinking habits
- ❏ Water, 14 gallons. (**Note:** If you live in an arid region, you'll need to store considerably more.)

RECOMMENDED BOOKS THAT
DEAL WITH FOOD STORAGE

* Layton, Peggy. *Emergency Food Storage & Survival Handbook: Everything You Need to Know to Keep Your Family Safe in a Crisis.* New York: Clarkson Potter/Crown Publishing, 2002.
* Layton, Peggy, and Vicki Tate. *Cookin' with Home Storage.* Self-published, 1991.

✔ *Today's Assignment:*

Make your shopping list for a year's supply of food and start adding the foods to your storage pantry. Most of you will need to space your buying over several weeks or even months, and that is fine. The important thing is that you get started. And remember that you also have to learn how to *cook* these types of unprocessed food, so fix a few meals using ingredients from your pantry.

Get a checkup

and build your

medical kit.

I ndividual health is an area many preppers overlook. You need to get regular medical and dental checkups; do at least moderate exercise, such as walking 30 minutes a day; eat a nutritious diet; maintain a healthy weight; and learn how to relax and get rid of stress.

If disaster strikes, being unhealthy will make it much more difficult to survive. Plus, being healthy can only make your everyday life better. Think about it . . . and then start a health-improvement program and stick to it. After a few weeks, it will become part of your normal routine, and you'll do it without consciously having to think about it.

Before you start, you need to find out where you stand healthwise. So today's assignment in your 31-day survival program is to make an appointment with a doctor for a complete checkup, including bloodwork.

I know—I don't like going to the doctor or giving blood either, but doing so will tell you a lot about your current health and will give you a baseline indicating where you need improvement. Look at it as a challenge to bring your health, weight, and vital numbers (e.g., blood pressure, cholesterol, triglycerides, blood sugar) in line with the recommended numbers.

If you're uninsured and your income is minimal, you can get a lot of health services from your local county health department, including immunizations. In the Denver area, one television station sponsors an annual health fair (and I assume there are similar programs all over) where you can get a complete blood workup up for a few bucks, with other screenings at nominal costs. Also check at local health clinics that treat uninsured patients on a sliding-scale basis.

You can do it. You just have to make up your mind and get it done.

After you get back from the doctor's office with a clean bill of health, it's time to start building your survival medical kit. Below, you'll find my suggestions about what should be included in such a kit, but keep in mind that these are only suggestions. The final contents will depend on your individual skills, needs, and budget. The books listed on pages 29 and 30 describe how to use many of these items in a medical emergency, as will the literature that comes with these items. Retain all boxes and instructional inserts.

SURVIVAL MEDICAL KIT

❏ Antibacterial soap
❏ Antidiarrhea medication
❏ Bandages and dressings (large)
❏ Basic surgical kit
❏ Bed liners or plastic sheeting
❏ Blood pressure monitor
❏ CPR shield
❏ Crutches, adjustable
❏ Epsom salts (makes a good laxative in a pinch)
❏ Examination gloves (preferably nonlatex), several boxes
❏ Eyeglasses (if applicable), extra pair
❏ Glucose monitor and test strips (even if you're not diabetic)
❏ Hearing aids and batteries (if applicable)
❏ Injectable antihistamine
❏ Injectable epinephrine
❏ IV electrolytes
❏ Laxatives
❏ Needles and silk thread if not in surgical kit

- ❏ Ophthalmic salve
- ❏ Oral and injectable antibiotics/sulfas
- ❏ Pain medications
- ❏ QuikClot clotting agent (some people prefer "Israeli battle dressings" for stopping bleeding)
- ❏ Razor or scalpel set
- ❏ Rubbing alcohol, peroxide, iodine, betadine (copious amounts)
- ❏ SAM splint
- ❏ Scissors
- ❏ Sterile IV kit
- ❏ Sterile needles and syringes
- ❏ Stethoscope
- ❏ Thermometer
- ❏ Tweezers

I recommend that folks get their eyes examined at least every three years. Older folks and those with hearing problems should get their hearing checked and pack extra hearing-aid batteries as suggested above.

☑ *Today's Assignment:*

Get a checkup. Buy the best basic first aid kit available at your local pharmacy and then expand the contents to include the items on the above list that are appropriate to your health needs and skill level.

Get your spouse

onboard for your

preparedness journey.

I'm lucky that I live by myself, with my girlfriend living in a nearby town. Marriage isn't a bad thing; in fact, marriage can be a wonderful gift if you have a compatible partner. Unfortunately, for many, the spouse may not be supportive of the partner's concerns and, in some instances, may even be hostile toward the whole concept of emergency preparedness.

At first, my girlfriend didn't know the extent of my preparations; she thought that I was just into living cheaply and preparing for bad weather and such. Over the past several months, I've slowly introduced her to more "extreme ideas" regarding long-term disaster preparedness.

If you're constantly fighting resistance from your spouse, you won't be able to sustain the required effort for the long haul. The way your spouse views your emergency-preparedness pursuits will be determined by the way he or she is affected by your efforts and where the spouse feels he/she fits into your priorities.

Here are some tips that should help keep your spouse happy and supportive of your efforts.

FIVE TIPS FOR BUILDING SUPPORT FOR YOUR PREPAREDNESS EFFORTS

1. *Set priorities.* Trust me; I know how easy it is to become totally obsessed with prepping, planning,

reading, and learning. This is necessary if you want to have a chance at surviving the coming mayhem; you just need to learn to set priorities. You may see collapse around every corner, but you should avoid constantly communicating your fears to your partner.

I'm not saying that you shouldn't mention potential threats or your plans to your partner; just don't talk about them all the time. If you do, he or she will quickly grow tired of your constant ramblings . . . and possibly of you. A good conversation ratio would be 95 percent sweet-talk and 5 percent doom and gloom.

2. *Communicate your reasons for prepping.* This may sound contradictory to point one above, but it is necessary if you want to get your spouse onboard. You just have to do it in the right way. Take it slow and try not to shock his or her senses or worldview too much at any given time.

For instance, say the two of you are watching the news, and the broadcaster gives an update on the current natural disaster (and there's always one somewhere in the world). Now would be a great time to ask your partner something like, "If something like that happened here, what would we do? Could we protect ourselves and our children?"

3. *Seek input from your spouse.* Try to get your partner involved in some way. Ask for opinions and suggestions. Encourage him or her to put together a bug-out bag in case a natural disaster happens in your area. No one can deny the fact that natural disasters do happen, and even the federal government recommends that everyone have an emergency kit . . .

4. *Watch movies.* As far as I'm concerned most movies are a waste of time, but the latest disaster flick could be a good way to help your partner visualize possible events and start thinking about the need to prepare. Again, don't shock the senses—a story line about a massive earthquake, tsunami, or tornado, for instance,

would have more influence than a zombie apocalypse. Try to keep it real and point out the need for you two to prepare for a similar event.

5. *Read books.* This can be a great way to break down the wall of resistance, especially if your significant other likes to read. Buy a book that deals with some aspect of survival—for example, *One Second After* by William R. Forstchen (don't overlook the instructional value in good fiction)—and give it as a present on a holiday or special occasion.

✔ *Today's Assignment:*

Come up with a list of things you can do to make you spouse more supportive of your preparedness plan. Resolve to make the activities fun as well as educational.

DAY 12

Learn to sprout seeds for fresh greens all year.

Fresh sprouts are full of vitamins and minerals that aren't readily available in the unsprouted seed. Sprouting allows you to have fresh greens even in winter and will expand the bulk of your food storage many times over without any extra expense to you.

To start sprouting, you'll need at least one wide-mouth quart canning jar (a quart mayonnaise jar will also work) and a 6x6-inch square piece of nylon window screen or cheesecloth. Both the screen and cheesecloth are easy to cut with scissors or a sharp knife.

Sprouts are easy to grow, safe, and nutritious.

Nylon window screen held in place by a metal canning jar ring.

Draining excess water from freshly soaked seeds.

Next, put approximately 3 to 4 ounces of wheat, alfalfa, chickpeas, lentils, mung beans, pumpkin seeds, rye, sunflower seeds, or other sprouting seed in each jar and cover the mouth with the nylon window screen. You can use a large rubber band, string, or a canning jar ring to hold the screen in place over the mouth of the jar.

Fill each jar with water to within 2 inches of the top and let stand overnight. When you get up the next morning, pour out the soak water and tilt the bottom of the jar over the sink and leave for an hour or two so the rest of the water can drain off the seeds.

After this initial soaking and draining, you'll want to flood the jars about every four hours and then drain any excess water by tilting the jar bottom up into a bowl or sink. Repeat two to three times per day. At this point, you want to keep the seeds moist but not covered with water.

In a few days, the seeds will begin to sprout. When the sprouts reach 1 to 2 inches in length (for most seeds), they are

After three days, sprouted seeds have filled the jar.

ready to eat. Sprouts can be eaten raw, cooked, or dried. If dried, they can be ground into flour and used for bread or other baked items.

To keep a steady supply of fresh sprouts, simply start a new jar 24 to 48 hours after the last sprout jar has finished sprouting. Repeat cycle. This is a great routine that will keep you in fresh greens year round.

And that is all there is to it.

If you want to learn more about sprouting, including in-depth but simple recipes using sprouts, order a copy of *The Sprouting Book* by Ann Wigmore. This excellent resource is a must-have for any serious survival seed sprouter.

Warning: Even though the risk is low, because sprouts can contain bacterial contamination, people with compromised immune systems (e.g., individuals with AIDS, organ transplants, undergoing chemotherapy) are advised to avoid eating them.

☑ *Today's Assignment:*

Use the method described above to sprout at least one batch of seeds.

Let's take a trip

to the hardware store.

Y ou need tools for building and repairing things, and you could easily spend several hundred dollars building a tool kit. It would be worth it, but most of us simply don't have that kind of money. Below you'll find the contents for both a basic and a bare-bones tool kit.

Most department/hardware stores will have everything you need to build a survival tool kit.

BASIC SURVIVAL TOOL KIT

- ❏ Adjustable wrenches, 6-inch and 18-inch
- ❏ Bolt cutters
- ❏ Bow saw
- ❏ Carpenter's string and chalk
- ❏ Chain saw, extra chains, two-cycle, spare parts, safety gear, chain oil, and chain files
- ❏ Claw hammer
- ❏ Crosscut saw
- ❏ Double-bit ax
- ❏ Duct tape, five or more rolls (might also consider one or more rolls of glass strapping tape)
- ❏ Electrical tape, five or more rolls
- ❏ Hand cleaner (waterless is best, for example GoJo)
- ❏ Hacksaw and extra pack of cutting blades
- ❏ Multitool
- ❏ Needle-nose pliers
- ❏ Round-nose pliers
- ❏ Rubber mallet
- ❏ Safety glasses
- ❏ Screwdriver set
- ❏ Shovel
- ❏ Single-jack hammer for starting wedges
- ❏ Sledgehammer
- ❏ Socket and ratchet set
- ❏ Spirit (or bubble) level; also line level
- ❏ Tape measure
- ❏ Teflon thread-sealing tape
- ❏ Wedge
- ❏ Wheelbarrow
- ❏ Wire (soft iron or copper)
- ❏ Wire cutters
- ❏ Wire strippers
- ❏ Wood-splitting maul, 8-pound
- ❏ Wood-splitting wedges (steel), two
- ❏ Work gloves (several pairs)

BARE-BONES SURVIVAL TOOL KIT

- ❏ Adjustable wrench, 6-inch
- ❏ Bow saw
- ❏ Claw hammer
- ❏ Duct tape, two rolls
- ❏ Flat-head and Phillips screwdrivers
- ❏ Hacksaw and extra blades
- ❏ Safety glasses
- ❏ Tape measure
- ❏ Vise grips
- ❏ Work gloves, extra pair

Note: Whenever you buy tools, get good-quality ones. Cheaply made brands won't last, and you may not be able to find replacement tools when you most need them. Plus, you'll end up spending more in the long run if you have to replace the tool because it broke or wasn't up to the task you needed it for. That doesn't mean that you have to buy the most expensive tools, however. Garage sales and flea markets are great sources for tools, and name-brand tools are often available at discount stores, such as K-mart or Walmart, as well as online.

☑ *Today's Assignment:*

Put together either a basic or bare-bones survival tool kit. It would be better for you to have the basic kit, but if you cannot do so now, assemble the bare-bones kit and supplement it as you can. (**Note:** Gardening tools are covered on day 23.)

DAY 14

Put together a bug-out bag.

Some people might consider a bug-out bag and a 72-hour kit as essentially the same thing. For the purposes of this book, I consider them as two separate kits. The 72-hour kit listed on day 6 is more of a "stay at home and ride out the short-term disaster" kit, while the bug-out bag described below is more of a "grab and go" kit.

The very idea of leaving the security of your home to "bug out" to the woods has never set well with me. In nearly every instance, it is better to hunker down or "bug in" than to bug out. Why leave the safety and familiar surroundings of your home for the open and unforgiving wilderness?

For many people, fleeing is their first line of preparation against disaster. Unfortunately, most will end up joining the multitude of other refugees freezing in a cave; dying from exposure, starvation, or violence at the hands of the mob; or becoming wards of whatever government entity is still functioning.

I live in a fairly safe area and have prepared to survive at home. I can conceive of only a few scenarios that would force me to leave. Even then, I would go to the house of an out-of-state relative with whom I have an agreement: if need be, he can come to my place or I can go to his after a disaster.

I know what you're thinking: what about an "end of the world as we know it" type of event? Well, if such an event does take place, there will be no 100 percent safe place for most of us anyway, and do you really think you would be better off trying to hide in the open wilderness than hunkering down at home?

Don't get me wrong—I'm *not* saying you should never bug out; you should keep all options open. What I am saying is that there are better ways to survive most disasters than heading into the bush.

You need to weigh the risks of bugging out vs. hunkering down and make your final decision based on logic and type of threat. That's the way decisions should be made. Unfortunately, when making survival decisions, many people rely on emotion (to run and hide) rather than more tried-and-true logic.

Relying on emotion instead of logic can make for some interesting adventures. However, without sound planning, those adventures are likely to be short-lived. For example, I recently asked a fellow in his late 30s what he would do if disaster struck his area. He thought for a moment and said he would gather his family and all the food, guns, and ammunition he could find and head for the mountains that lie some 75 miles north of his home.

Depending on the type of disaster, his "plan" might work short-term for a lone survivor or a small group of individuals in good physical condition and equipped with proper gear and mindset. But he is the father of a newborn, and his wife thinks missing an appointment at the nail salon is the end of the world as she knows it. Making matters worse, the young father has no outdoor survival training or skills other than watching reruns of Les Stroud's *Survivorman* television show and camping at a national park campground with all the utilities and hookups provided. Why he thinks he can survive in the wilderness while dragging his young family along, I don't know. He isn't thinking logically, and if he ever has to put his plan to the test during a real emergency, his family will likely suffer or possibly even die.

Unfortunately, this "batman in the boondocks" mentality will continue to be the chosen survival plan for many who haven't thought survival through logically and come up with a realistic plan.

When making survival plans for your family, you have to

honestly weigh the risks of your decision based on logic. In almost every disaster scenario, it is better to stay put (bugging in) or head to a prearranged safe place at an out-of-town relative's or friend's house than it is to head to the woods to eat twigs and pine bark.

Therefore, for most people an evacuation bag is a better choice than a bug-out bag. An evacuation bag should contain the gear necessary to get you from point A to point B, whereas a bug-out bag (in most cases) is geared more toward wilderness survival. I have both, but admittedly my bug-out bag is an option of last resort.

Knowing *when* to go is much more important than the contents of your survival pack or even where you will go. You don't want to jump and run before you need to, but if you wait too long you may never reach your destination. If you wait for the authorities to give the order to evacuate, it may already be too late. The roads leading to safety could be blocked or impassable by motor vehicle, and walking to your destination may be impossible or too dangerous to attempt.

On the other hand, if you jump and run in response to every potential disaster, you'll soon deplete your resources and the patience of your family, school, and employers. For example, say you live in an area prone to tornadoes, like Texas, and you evacuate to Arkansas (which has also suffered its share of killer tornados over the years) every time the clouds turn dark or the wind shakes the leaves. You would be on the road nonstop during tornado season—which seems to be most of the time in Texas. But waiting until the twister is at your door will also put you at an unnecessary risk.

There are no easy answers. All you can do is weigh the dangers of bugging out vs. hunkering down logically based on the situation at hand. You have to consider the nature of the threat and ask yourself which option gives you the better chance of surviving the type of disaster you are facing.

Of course, there are times when evacuation is a no-brainer. Say, for example, you live on the Florida coast and a category 5 hurricane has been predicted to hit your area within 72 hours.

In that case, you would be foolish not to go as soon as possible, even if you have no prearranged bug-out location.

On the other hand, let's say there is a snowstorm heading your way and you have food, water, heat, and a way to cook even if the power goes out for an extended time. Then you are probably better off to hunker down where you are.

In my opinion, the bugging out vs. hunkering down debate is moot because it all comes down to the type of threat you face, your personal situation, and your preparedness level. In the end, you'll have to decide what to do on a case-by-case basis.

BUG-OUT BAG CONTENTS

Please note that the following list is intended only as a suggestion. Your bug-out bag should be customized to suit your individual needs, plans, and location.

❏ Antibacterial hand wipes
❏ Cash—$100 in ones, fives, and tens
❏ Cell phone and charger
❏ Change of clothes
❏ First aid tactical trauma kit
❏ Fishing kit
❏ Fixed-blade knife
❏ GPS navigator (handheld)
❏ Handgun and 200 + rounds of ammunition
❏ LED flashlight (small) with extra batteries, as well as a crank-type flashlight that doesn't require batteries
❏ Lighters (small), two
❏ Map of area (detailed) and compass
❏ Multitool
❏ OC spray
❏ Para cord, 25 feet
❏ Prepaid calling card
❏ Prescription medications, as needed
❏ Sewing kit (small)
❏ Space blanket

❑ Sterno folding stove
❑ Trail mix, box of energy bars (15), and electrolyte packets
❑ Wooden matches in a waterproof container
❑ Water filter or bottle

Note: If forced to bug out by car, load both your 72-hour kit and bug-out bags.

SPECIAL CONSIDERATIONS FOR CHILDREN

In stressful situations, it is important for you to appear relaxed, confident, and in control—even if you are a trembling bag of nerves on the inside. The last thing children need is extra stress brought on by a panicked parent.

Another consideration concerning children is familiarity. During a bug-out situation, you will be away from home, and this can be extremely stressful for children. It is important to eliminate as much of the stress as possible. One way to do this is by bringing along items that are familiar to them. If they have a favorite blanket, pillow, stuffed toy, or other object that comforts them, be sure to pack it before heading out the door. This is very important.

Children tend to bore easily, so adding items to forestall or extinguish their boredom will make the time away from home much easier for all of you. You may want to put together a pack just for them consisting of toys, books, cards, writing/drawing materials, and games. Don't forget extra batteries for those games and toys that need them. Of course, children aren't the only ones who get bored; include things that will keep your boredom in check as well.

✔ *Today's Assignment:*

Put together your bug-out bag, as well as a separate one for your children if applicable.

DAY 15

Let's go shopping for basic survival supplies.

Today, you'll be taking another trip to your local discount or hardware store for basic survival supplies. Now you are building on the stuff you assembled for your 72-hour kit on Day 6. Again, the list below isn't written in stone; it should be tailored to meet your individual needs.

❏ Batteries for the flashlights, radio, and head lamps (at least 24 sets)
❏ Cigarette lighters, 12
❏ Diapers and other supplies for infants (e.g., baby wipes, rash cream, bottles, nipples, pacifiers, baby toiletries)
❏ Feminine-hygiene supplies, approximately 500 count per female in your group
❏ Fire extinguishers, two per household
❏ Food storage bags (e.g., Ziploc), five boxes, various sizes
❏ LED flashlights, two
❏ LED headlamps, two
❏ Matches (wooden), five boxes
❏ Playing cards and several board games (avoid battery-powered games)
❏ Propane stove (two-burner) and 12 one-pound propane cylinders (**Note:** A dual-fuel model increases versatility.)
❏ Radio, AM/FM
❏ Razor blades (double-edged), 100. (**Note:** If you don't have a

razor, you may have to order one, and don't forget a brush and bowl.)

- ❏ Soap (bath), 12 bars per person
- ❏ Soap (dishwashing), 12 bottles
- ❏ Toilet paper, as much as you can reasonably store
- ❏ Toothbrushes, 12 per person in your group
- ❏ Toothpaste, 6 large tubes per person in your group
- ❏ Trash bags (28-gallon), five 28-count boxes
- ❏ Wool socks and thermal underwear, three pairs per person

✔ *Today's Assignment:*

Head to the store and assemble your basic survival package.

Build a box trap.

No doubt many of you have read about various improvised and homemade traps in one of the many outdoor survival books and thought, *Wow, what a great idea—I could do that.* Indeed, many of the ideas and diagrams shown are ingenious, and a few of them actually work to trap game—with practice.

After seeing all these trap designs in these books, you might think you need to learn how to make them all yourself, or that these homemade traps are somehow more proficient than commercially manufactured traps at putting food on the table or keeping pests out of your garden. You don't, and they're not.

The main (and possibly only) advantage homemade traps have over most of their store-bought counterparts is that they can be built from scrounged materials. That is a huge advantage and the reason you should learn how to make several different types of do-it-yourself traps. But don't go overboard here or discount a factory-made trap as somehow inferior for survival because you did not carve it out of three twigs that are held together by a strand of your own hair.

Generally, factory-made traps are superior to most homemade designs, and you should take full advantage of their use. When you are planning for survival, the last thing you want to do is limit yourself in any way. The best course of action is to blend primitive techniques and tools with modern advancements, therefore increasing your chances of survival.

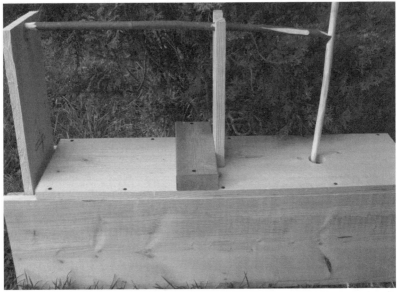

Simple, homemade box traps, such as this one, are very effective for trapping small game.

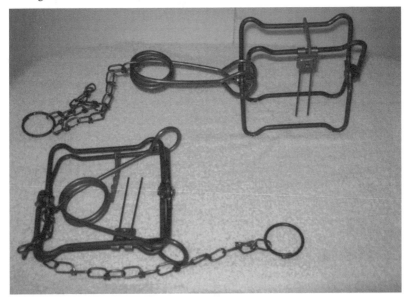

The #110 Conibear body trap is the best commercially manufactured trap for catching small game.

For best results when trapping small game, I recommend that you invest in a good supply (at least 10 traps, with 20 or more being ideal) of #110 Conibear body traps. They are easy to use for most people and are very effective for filling the stew pot. Plus, they are quick-kill traps and are therefore more humane.

With that said, the best homemade trap for the average survivor is the wooden box or cage trap, as they are commonly called. I am sure most of you have seen or heard about the live traps made by Havahart (www.havahart.com). These traps are lightweight (compared to the homemade version illustrated here) and work great, but they're expensive, running upwards of $30 for the smallest trap. Sizes for larger animals, such as raccoon, can cost $100 or more depending on the retailer.

I didn't have the money to purchase several of these traps, and it didn't make good economic sense to do so anyway, since I could make as many as I need for little or nothing. Box traps are cheap and easy to build using plywood or scrap lumber that can easily be found while scavenging through construction site Dumpsters or around abandoned structures or other locations in the country.

These traps are easy on the critters trapped inside, unlike other traps that rely on killing or maiming to secure the animal. An added plus is that game caught in a box trap is kept safe from hungry predators until the trapper returns to check the trap.

When I was growing up in the Appalachian Mountains of Tennessee, just about every boy knew how to build a homemade box trap out of scrap wood. Now kids are more interested in watching TV or playing video games than learning such useful skills. This is sad, because one day this type of skill could make the difference between going to bed hungry or on a full stomach.

To construct this trap, begin by putting together a box using outdoor plywood, lumber, or other suitable material. Each end is left open and should be approximately 6 or 12 inches square, depending on the intended game.

The top piece should be 2 or 3 inches shorter on one end— or if you intend to build a trap with double doors, make the top piece 2 or 3 inches shorter at *both* ends—which will allow room for the sliding door(s).

BUILD A BOX TRAP   **67**

Top view showing the slideway for the door and the top of the trap.

For larger animals, such as raccoon, opossum, and wood-chuck, the box should be at least 36 inches long and have at least a 12-inch doorway. For smaller game, such as squirrels, rabbits, muskrat, and mink, a 24-inch box with a 6-inch opening works well.

You have to construct a slideway for the doors to fall through and lock in. You can make the trigger system out of branches or other improvised materials. Explaining here in writing how the pieces go together is difficult, but it should all be clear when you look at the photos.

Use the heaviest wood you can find for the doors, as the weight will cause them to close faster and go all the way down and lock into place when the trigger is tripped.

Close-up view of key trigger points that hold the door in the open position until dislodged by an animal, at which time they collapse, dropping the door and trapping the animal inside.

HOW TO USE THESE TRAPS

Most traps of this type are set with bait. If you are baiting for raccoon, use peanut butter or fish guts; for opossums, use cut-up apples, peanut butter, or just about anything with a strong odor. Cats like fish guts; squirrels like acorns and corn; pheasants and quail like wheat or crushed dried corn. When in doubt, use a spoonful of peanut butter, as most animals seem to be attracted to it.

Many of us who keep chickens know how frustrating it is to watch our prized hens disappear one at a time to a seemingly invisible predator. Catching the phantom culprit can be a bewildering problem, since in many cases we don't know exactly what we are trying to catch or when it will make its next foray into the henhouse.

I keep two of these traps set and against the outside walls of my henhouse. I conceal the traps with hay to look like a naturally occurring run or passage and usually catch several would-be chicken thieves (mostly raccoons) each month. They seem to just meander into the traps while searching for a way inside the coop.

A dandy rabbit-producing method is to set out boxes in known rabbit country, with brush piled on top of the trap to make it look like a natural hiding place. Make sure that the brush you use doesn't interfere with the trigger assembly or keep the door from closing all the way.

I like to funnel the rabbits into the trap by placing "wings" made from scrap lumber in a V pattern that lead from the entrance of the traps. This seems to guide the animals naturally into the traps. These winged traps do not even have to be baited; the rabbits just wander into them while looking for a place to hide. Be patient: don't expect to catch anything in the first couple of weeks. The rabbits need to become accustomed to seeing the traps before they will start to come in.

If you can find a copy, I suggest you buy *Being Kind to Animal Pests: A No-Nonsense Guide to Humane Animal Control with Cage Traps* by Steve Meyer (the book is out of print, but new and used copies can be purchased from Amazon and other online booksellers). It is a great guide to using this type of trap effectively.

Today's Assignment:

Build one or more box traps designed to capture the type of animals you want to serve for dinner or keep out of your garden or henhouse.

DAY 17

Get a dental checkup and put together a dental first aid kit.

The health of your teeth is directly linked to the health of your body, and being unhealthy when disaster strikes will make it much more difficult to survive. Plus, being healthy—whether or not an emergency arises—will improve the quality of your life now and make you more productive.

Make an appointment with your dentist for a checkup and get any dental problems taken care of. It's better to get it done now with proper dental care than later by Uncle Bob with a pair of pliers and a gulp of homebrew for pain.

Even if you've taken all the proper precautions, dental emergencies do happen, and you need to be ready with the necessary tools and know-how to fix the problem. So, after your dental checkup, the next parts of your assignment are to put together a dental first aid kit and obtain the knowledge to use it properly.

SURVIVAL DENTAL KIT

❑ Clove oil (a natural pain reliever)
❑ Cotton
❑ Dental mirror
❑ Dental pain reliever (e.g., Orajel)
❑ Dental pick
❑ Dental wax

- Exam gloves (nonlatex, as some people are allergic to latex; try nitrile or rubber)
- Gauze
- Hand sanitizer
- Ibuprofen (e.g., Advil or Motrin) to relieve pain and inflammation
- Temporary filling material (e.g., Temparin or Cavit)
- Toothpicks
- Tweezers

Of course, you should stock up on the basics: toothpaste, floss, and brushes. Buy extra since in a long-term, grid-down situation, these make great barter items. As recommended earlier, I encourage you to get a copy of *Where There Is No Dentist*, available at amazon.com or Hesperian.org (where it is also available as a downloadable title).

✔ *Today's Assignment:*

Get a thorough checkup from your dentist, have any dental problems fixed, assemble a dental emergency kit, and learn how to use the items in it.

W hen asked where they should start their survival
preparations, most people answer food storage. *Wrong.*
In fact, food isn't even in the top three survival priorities. The most important elements of survival are oxygen, shelter from extreme weather, and water.

Depending on health, physical activity, and environment,
and with limited activity, humans can survive:

❑ Five minutes or less without oxygen
❑ 10 days or fewer without water at 50°F (and even fewer
as temperatures rise)
❑ Four to six weeks without food

Today's task involves making sure your survival plan
includes a reliable source of clean water. Imagine how disap-
pointed you'd be after investing all that time and money to build
your stockpile of survival food only to realize that you were
about to die of dehydration because you neglected to adequately
address your need for water. Having food storage without a reliable source of clean water is like eating soup with a fork. You're
only getting some of what you need.

Before getting started, a few words on terminology are in
order. Sometimes the terms *filtration*, *purification*, and *sterilization* are used interchangeably in relation to water. This is

This homemade water filter works as well as any commercial model and costs considerably less.

incorrect. *Filtration* removes solid matter (or in some cases emulsified liquids). *Purification* removes that which is not water (stuff in solution and/or emulsion). *Sterilization* kills microbes in the water. The confusion of terms is understandable, as many commercial filter units also remove microbes by filtering them out, and many units include activated charcoal or other elements that both filter out solids and remove a lot of metals in solution by adsorption (as opposed to absorption). In fact, they now have filters that are so specific and so fine they actually can filter out molecules: a "watermaker" that filters out salt from seawater would be an example.

I'm a fan of the Berkey water filters. Having used a Big Berkey filter extensively for more than three years, I can personally attest to its performance. However, a lot of people can't or won't spend $250 or more for a water filter no matter how critical it is to their survival. Fortunately, it isn't difficult to make your own homemade water filter using only the Black Berkey Purification Elements and a few odds and ends you probably have lying around your house. The total cost for such a unit at the time of this writing is less than $150, including the Black Berkey Purification Elements.

Black Berkey Purification Elements can be ordered online from a number of vendors, including Amazon.com and LPC Survival (www.directive21.com), with current prices ranging from $99 to $110. I've found LPC Survival to be very reliable, with superfast shipping and great customer service.

WHAT YOU'LL NEED

- ❑ Two Black Berkey Purification Elements
- ❑ Two 5-gallon food-grade buckets with lids
- ❑ Food-grade spigot (available at most hardware stores or online; the type used for large water coolers works great)
- ❑ Drill with 1/2- and 3/4-inch bits

First drill two 1/2-inch holes in the bottom of one of the buckets and two 3/4-inch holes through one of the lids. The holes

Black Berkey Purification Elements secured through the bottom of the top bucket using 1/2-inch holes and supplied wingnuts. Note how the elements protrude through the bottom of the top bucket and align with the holes through the lid of the bottom bucket.

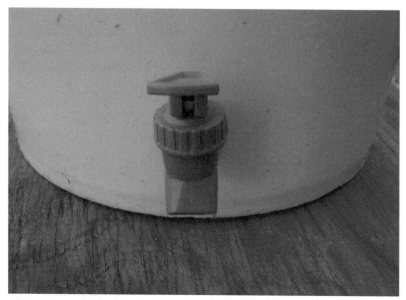

This spigot was taken from a busted water cooler.

should be approximately 4 to 6 inches apart to facilitate changing the filters as needed. Both sets of holes in the bottom of the bucket and those in the lid should match up perfectly when mated.

Next, drill a 3/4-inch hole in the side of the other bucket. This hole is for the spigot, so drill about 2 inches up from the bottom of the bucket. This way when it is set on a table or bench, the spigot isn't touching the surface, where it can be damaged or broken.

Install the Black Berkey Purification Elements securely through the 1/2-inch holes that you drilled in the bottom of the first bucket, using the supplied rubber washers and wingnut fasteners. Be careful not to overtighten the nuts or you could cause a leak or even break the tip of a purification element.

To use this unit, put the lid with the 1/2-inch holes on top of the bucket with the spigot and set the other bucket with the filters installed on top, aligning the holes so the Berkey filter tubes extend through the lid of the lower bucket.

Pour the water to be filtered into the upper bucket and cover with the remaining lid. The water in the top bucket will drip through the filter elements and into the lower bucket, filling it with clean drinking water.

As you can see from the photos, it's very simple. The whole process takes about 20 minutes.

WATER PURIFICATION

After filtration, water can be purified through various means, including adding household bleach, boiling it, and using the SODIS (solar water disinfecting) method.

Bleach

If you suspect the water contains contaminants, add eight drops of regular, unscented, liquid household bleach (e.g., Purex, Clorox) to each gallon of water, stir it well, and let it stand for 30 minutes before drinking.

Boiling

Boiling is one of the surest methods of water purification. All you need is a heat source, a suitable container, and water. Bring the water to a *rolling boil* to kill any contaminants that may be present. Boiled water tastes like, well, boiled water, but the taste can be somewhat improved by pouring back and forth between two containers to reoxygenate.

SODIS Method

Clean a transparent polyethylene terephthalate (PET) bottle (e.g., soda bottle) with soap and water. Then fill the bottle with the water to be disinfected and place the bottle in full sunlight for at least six hours.

Note: It is the ultraviolet rays from the sun, and not heat, that kill the waterborne pathogens. Go to www.sodis.ch/methode/an-wendung/index_EN for detailed instructions and illustrations.

WATER STORAGE

For water storage, I have six 5-gallon containers bought in the sporting goods department at Walmart. Thirty gallons of water isn't much, but I don't see water being a major issue at my location. If you live in a drier region, such as the American southwest, water will likely be a major concern, which may necessitate the storage of hundreds or even thousands of gallons for an extended emergency.

Don't store water in used 5-gallon milk jugs. They're not strong enough for long-term storage and eventually break down and leak. The 5-gallon containers sold in the sporting goods section of most department or hardware stores work great, as do the 55-gallon plastic water drums sold by preparedness gear retailers, such as Emergency Essentials at BePrepared.com.

If you must use small containers, empty 2-liter soda bottles work well. They are stronger than milk jugs, have better lids, and are more convenient. Avoid glass containers because they break too easily.

TAP WATER CONSIDERATIONS

If you're storing tap water from a municipal water system, there's no need to add bleach as suggested by some. Water from the municipal tap already contains enough chlorine to thwart any bacterial growth, so it can be stored without any other additives.

Today's Assignment:

Construct a water purifier and educate yourself about water purification and storage.

Avoid these 10

prepping mistakes.

Below are 10 common mistakes I've seen survival planners make over the years (I've made several of them myself), and I don't want you to end up doing the same.

1. *Giving up too early.* Many new survivalists start out with a lot of energy and enthusiasm, only to give up before meeting their goals. The main reason: they think they have to spend thousands of dollars on a retreat, survival food, and a weapons arsenal. Since they don't have the money, they give up altogether.

2. *Procrastinating.* Don't put off starting your preparedness program. The number-one excuse given is a lack of money—see point 1 above.

3. *Not making their own plan.* Many new survivalists, not knowing where to start, attempt to follow the plans of others. Granted, there will be a lot of similarities between most survival plans, but it is important to look at your location, needs, and budget, and plan accordingly.

4. *Overlooking the need for shelter.* Many new (and veteran) survivalists fail to realize the importance of a paid-for plot of land and shelter. They seem to think that their debt will miraculously disappear or be forgiven. Sorry, folks, it doesn't work that way. My book *Dirt Cheap Survival Retreat* (available from Paladin

Press) gives a complete plan for setting up a paid-for survival retreat on a paid-for plot of land with very little cash.

5. *Planning to bug out.* Bugging out can work if you have a place to go and can make it there unscathed. But the "throw on a pack and live in the woods" plan is unrealistic and impractical. Some may be able to pull it off—most won't.

6. *Investing in too many guns.* Firearms are very important, but many new (and veteran) survivalists have more guns than pounds of wheat. Get the life-sustaining basics squared away first.

7. *Buying books but not reading them.* I'm sure many of you do this. You read a review of a preparedness book and immediately send for it. When it arrives in the mail, you open the package, thumb through it, and think, *I'll read it when I have more time.* And on the shelf it goes, where it does you no good.

8. *Buying books but not doing what they teach.* Some people actually read the books, but that's as far as it goes. They never go out and test what they've read. Reading is great, but you need to get off the couch and put what you've read into practice.

9. *Not planning for unexpected arrivals.* What will you do when unexpected visitors arrive at your door looking for a handout post collapse? It is a good idea to buy extra food and assemble care packages now.

10. *Having a closed mind.* Some people become fixated with their plans (or the plans of others—see point 3). If something works, great; if not, you need to find out what the problem is and fix it, even if it means a complete overhaul of your original plan.

✔ Today's Assignment:

Do a self-evaluation (be honest), keeping the 10 points above in mind. If you find you're guilty of making any of the mistakes listed, then get to work correcting the issues.

Take a firearms

safety and/or

hunter education class.

M any of you probably have at least a basic knowledge of firearms safety and shooting fundamentals. If not, then I suggest you seek out qualified instruction to acquire those skills _before_ buying a gun. The National Rifle Association offers fundamental classes as well as more advanced training. For more information about the classes, see the NRA website: www.nra.org/programs.aspx.

Other possible options are hunter-education classes offered by the wildlife or natural resources agencies in most states. These classes are usually free to anyone (at least in every state I checked) and are a good starting point for learning general firearms safety and handling, as well as a few basic outdoor survival skills. Best of all, the classes can be a lot of fun. Contact your state's appropriate agency for information and class schedules.

Most states also offer concealed-carry permit classes; as of this writing, these classes cost around $50 to attend and last eight to ten hours. Most cover general handgun safety, care, responsibility, and laws regarding firearms and self-defense in the sponsoring state. Contact your state's department of public safety or whatever the relevant agency is called in your state for information about class schedules.

Once you have the basics mastered and can shoot well enough to place all your shots into a 6-inch circle or less at 25 yards, then it is time to broaden your skills. If attending a

A .22-caliber revolver is an excellent choice for new handgun shooters to learn how to shoot safely.

dedicated defensive-shooting course is possible, what are you waiting for? Do it. Be sure to check the instructor's credentials before signing up for the course. For example, just because someone was once a police officer or in the military doesn't always make hin a good shooting instructor. Consult others who have taken firearms instruction and see what they have to say.

If attending a dedicated defensive course isn't possible, then instructional DVDs are a good alternative. Paladin Press offers hundreds of this type of instructional videos, and I recommend the offerings by Kelly McCann and his Crucible team. His *Defensive Shooting Series* video is excellent. (**Note:** The byline on the *Defensive Shooting Series* DVD is Jim Grover because at the time McCann was using that pseudonym for his published works.)

With the cost of ammo going through the roof, practicing with live ammo can be a wallet-flattening ordeal. Sure we need to use live rounds in training, but a lot of realistic and constructive practice can be done with CO_2 powered pistols, which are sold in most sporting goods and department stores.

Another advantage of this type of training is that it can be done in your backyard, even in town, if you have a good fence to keep your activities private and materials to set up a proper, safe backstop. Your practice can even be undertaken in a basement or extra room if needed. Just remember to make it as realistic as possible and always reinforce what you learn with live fire when possible.

☑ *Today's Assignment:*

Find the nearest firearms-related class, sign up, and make sure you show up for class.

Let's make a
small-game snare.

Snares can be used to trap a variety of animals from mice to elephants, and no survival book would be complete without plans for making and setting a snare. Since, I don't think many of you will be snaring elephants (or mice), we'll concentrate our efforts here on making and setting a snare sized for rabbits and squirrels. However, most of the same principles work just as well for smaller and larger animals.

Effective snares can be improvised from any pliable wire, cable, string, or rope, but in my opinion the best material for making a small-game snare is appliance wire. I get mine for free from discarded appliances found at the local dump, but you can also buy the wire at any hardware store for a few cents per foot.

To start, take a piece of wire 20 inches long and split it down the center, leaving you with two 20-inch pieces. Next, peel the rubber insulation back about 2 inches and use pliers to pull the wire out of the insulation. It may be necessary to split the insulation with a sharp knife before the wire and the rubber insulation can be separated.

The goal is to pull the copper wire free from the insulation in such a way that the strands don't unravel and tangle when pulled free. Don't worry if you have trouble the first few times; you'll get better with practice.

Once you have the wire and insulation separated, cut the ends off the wire evenly. Then measure a section 3 inches long

A small-game snare connected to a spring pole via a peg and nail trigger.

from one end and tightly wrap this around a small twig (slightly larger than the wire) or matchstick, forming a small loop. Now break and remove the stick, opening up the loop. Take the other end of the wire and pass it through the loop you just made, forming a lasso.

At the other end of the wire, opposite the lasso, securely tie another small loop. This will be used to secure the snare to a longer line or string. Now, you're probably asking why not just use a string in the first place, thus avoiding the wire altogether? Well, you could do that, but wire makes a much better snare for a number of reasons but mainly because it holds its shape when set.

Another possibility, if you want to make some up ahead of time and disperse through your various kits and bags, is to go to a fishing shop that caters to fishers of large fish (e.g., deep sea, steelhead), which will have lovely steel line, factory eyelets, and swivels that make great snares. A thin, stiff wire (aka wire leader) makes a great snare because it is inclined to cut the throat of whatever it has caught on the first lunge as it tightens.

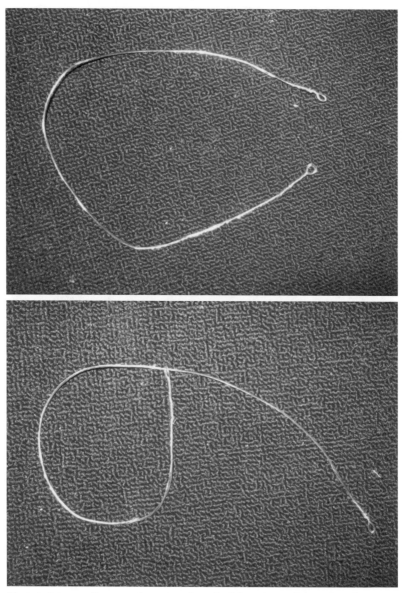

First, twist a small, secure loop at each end of the wire and then thread one end through the other.

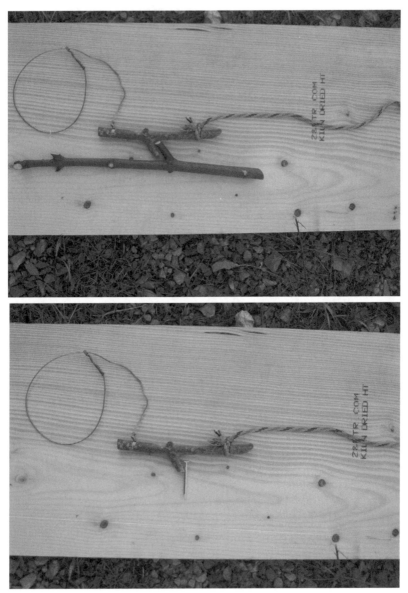

Two different trigger designs that can be used to connect the snare to a spring pole, which will lift the animal into the air when the trigger is tripped.

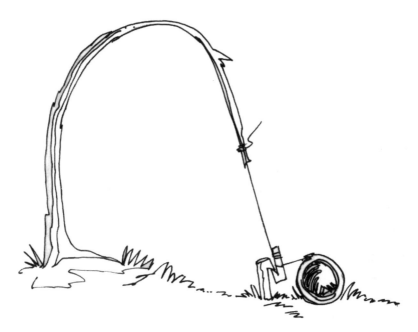

Twitch-up snare.

This gives nicely bled-out meat. These are sometimes used where deer jump a fence in the brush at the same spot all the time. This type usually does not require a spring-lift arrangement, as larger game will lunge as soon as they think they may be caught, doing themselves in by tightening the noose. Some poachers are rumored to use aircraft cable for larger animals.

✔ *Today's Assignment:*

Make a small-game snare using appliance wire. For more information about this topic, read *Into The Primitive: Advanced Trapping Techniques* by Dale Martin (available from Paladin Press).

22

Prevent and manage stress.

There is no such thing as a stress-free life. Most of us deal with stress on a daily basis, from getting the kids off to school on time to driving to work in rush-hour traffic to taking care of a sick family member.

Our bodies were designed to deal with stress on a short-term basis and then to relax and recuperate before facing the next stressful event. Our reaction to short-term stress is a "fight or flight" response, which in the past was necessary for our survival (and still is, depending on the situation).

Short-term stress doesn't have the same effect on our bodies as extended periods of tension and stress do; most healthy people can deal with stress without developing any long-term problems. It's those periods of long-term stress that we need to be concerned with, which is precisely what we would face during an extended emergency or grid-down situation.

During a prolonged emergency, our stress levels will naturally rise, possibly affecting both our physical and mental health and judgment. For this reason, it is important to know what stress does to your body and how to manage it so that it doesn't become a problem in a survival situation or in everyday life.

WHAT LONG-TERM STRESS DOES TO YOUR BODY

According to medical authorities, when you're stressed the

brain's sympathetic nerves signal the adrenal glands to release a number of chemicals into the body, including epinephrine (aka, adrenaline) and cortisol. Persistently high levels of these chemicals can impair memory and the ability to learn, which can inadvertently lead to mistakes. Mistakes can be deadly.

Stress triggers the body to produce extra blood sugar, which provides energy to power our innate fight-or-flight response. In some instances this is a good thing, but if your stress is prolonged, such as would be the case during a long-term survival situation, raised glucose levels may over time turn you into a full-blown diabetic, especially if you are already at risk.

Long-term stress can lead to cardiovascular problems, especially if you're already at risk due to lifestyle or heredity. Stress can raise blood pressure and over time[, lead to narrowing of the arteries and raised cholesterol levels, which increase your chances of heart disease, heart attack, and stroke. Ongoing stress can cause a loss of sleep, thus weakening your immune system and decreasing your body's ability to fight off infection and heal itself.

Stress can cause indigestion and nausea, possibly leading to diarrhea or constipation. This can lead to a loss of appetite or dehydration, both of which can cause other health problems.

TIPS FOR MANAGING STRESS

Below are 10 tips that I've found effective for dealing with stress. I hope you can adopt some of these strategies to help you manage stress now, as well as "after the balloon goes up."

1. *Be prepared.* Need, I say more? Being prepared is the most effective way of dealing with stress during and after a disaster or TEOTWAWKI (the end of the world as we know it). Nothing beats being prepared. While everyone else is running in circles, you can relax and watch the show. But you have to start.
2. *Take vitamin B-complex.* Supplementing with B-complex can play an important role in stress reduc-

tion. In addition to B-complex, passionflower and skullcap may help to relieve stress and improve sleep patterns. I take a tablet that has all three in one capsule. Ask your doctor first and start with a small dosage.

3. *Get enough sleep.* While I can't say for sure how long before you or I would die without sleep, it is a medical fact that a lack of sleep can wreak havoc on your health and mental functioning. I've gone several days without sleep, and my mental functions, coordination, and reaction times were definitely subpar. No matter what type of disaster you face or how bad things are, you have to sleep.

4. *Try valerian supplements.* Valerian has been used for centuries for treating nervous conditions, sleeplessness, epilepsy, depression, and hysteria. I've taken valerian supplements during periods of insomnia, and they work well. Other dietary supplements or herbal remedies frequently taken to aid in sleep include melatonin and chamomile. With any supplement, ask your doctor before taking and start with a small dose until you know how your body will react.

5. *Keep some semblance of normalcy.* This may sound nonsensical, but try to keep your life as normal as possible during these anything but normal times. For example, if you read before going to bed and work out in the morning, continue to do so. By keeping a familiar schedule, your mind and body will be better able to deal with the stress caused by a long-term disaster.

6. *Entertain yourself.* By keeping your mind busy during periods of downtime, you can limit stress and its negative effects on your body. I have a plastic tote full of unread (by me at least) paperback books that I've picked up at yard sales and flea markets for 10–20 cents each. Altogether they probably cost me less than $25 total, and they will provide invaluable entertainment value post collapse (or before). I also enjoy lis-

tening to music and have a number of CDs and rechargeable batteries to keep the music playing.

7. *Keep children happy.* If the kids aren't happy, then no one is happy. It is important to eliminate as much stress and unfamiliarity from their lives as possible, especially at first while they adjust. Children tend to bore easily, so adding things to your cache to stave off their boredom is a good idea. As mentioned earlier, you should have a special pack just for kids consisting of toys, books, and games. Don't forget extra batteries for electronics.

8. *Meditate.* Long used for stress reduction and as a means of relaxation, meditation involves clearing your mind of what is around you while focusing on proper breathing techniques to reach a calm state. See the online article "Benefits and Different Types of Meditation Techniques" (stress.about.com/od/low-stresslifestyle/a/meditation.htm) on the About.com website for more information and techniques on this subject.

9. *Pray.* If you are religious, prayer can be a great help for relieving stress and instilling a feeling of well-being and hope. Here is the best example I've ever read of a prayer to help you deal with stress (sorry, but I can't remember the original source):

"Lord, I pray that you provide me your hand and walk me through the dark times. I ask that you reduce the burdens in my life or show me the path to get things done or rid myself of the things weighing me down. Thank you, Lord, for all you do in my life and how you will provide for me, even in these stressful times."

✓ Today's Assignment:

Learn how to control your stress level. Trust me—this is one of the most important parts of your preparedness plan.

L et's face it: we cannot realistically store enough food to last for the rest of our lives (unless, of course, that life is very short). That is where such skills as hunting, trapping, foraging, raising livestock, and gardening come into play in the total survival food plan.

The most common excuse I hear for not planting a survival garden is that the person lacks either time or space or both. A lack of time or space can be challenging, but if done right planting a garden doesn't require a lot of either. We've already discussed how to prioritize to use time more efficiently, and gardening isn't that time consuming if done properly.

Regarding space, most people have more than they think; they just need to look at their situation from a different angle. When I lived in the city, I successfully raised tomatoes and other vegetables in a window box and in several hanging baskets on the terrace. Remember, even a small garden is better than no garden at all, and starting small has several advantages: less space required, less expense to get started, less time involved, and perhaps, most important, a chance to obtain the skills needed to eventually plant and grow a full-size garden if space permits.

TOOLS NEEDED

Contrary to what you might think, you don't need a lot of expensive tools to plant and tend a garden. My most important

A few good gardening and food-preservation books, as well as a supply of non-hybrid seeds, should be on every substance gardener's shopping list.

recommendations when buying tools are to buy the best tools you can afford and to choose forged tools over stamped ones. Even though top-quality forged tools cost more, they last considerably longer and make the job of gardening much easier.

The tools needed will depend on several factors, such as your location and what, how, and how much you intend to grow. At a bare minimum, I suggest a peasant hoe (also called an eye hoe), regular garden hoe, mattock, pitchfork, rake, digging shovel, classic round-point shovel, and digging fork.

WHAT TO GROW

Plant what grows well in your area. How do you know what crops thrive where you live? Well, the best way is to ask people:

talk to local gardeners, vendors at farmers market stalls or roadside stands, employees at nearby nurseries and seed stores, and staff members at your local county extension agency or farmers co-op. A wealth of information can be gained just by asking.

U.S. Department of Agriculture (USDA) climate zone maps provide a rough estimate as to what will grow best in your area of the country and planting guidelines. Every seed catalog I've seen has this type of climate zone map printed on the first couple of pages, or you can find one with a simple online search.

CHOOSING SEEDS

When it comes to gardening, you obviously must start with seeds, and the one question I'm asked most often pertaining to survival gardening is, "Should I choose hybrid or nonhybrid seeds?" My answer is always the same: both.

Seed from nonhybrid ("heirloom") varieties can be saved from one year to the next and will grow true to the parent plants. Hybrid varieties tend to grow more vigorously the first planting and are easier to grow, but saved seeds are unpredictable at best.

I suggest you start with hybrid seeds and proceed to growing nonhybrid varieties exclusively as your gardening skill improves. But with any seeds, you need to actually plant them, tend the plants, and watch them grow before you can learn or reap the harvest. One of the biggest mistakes I see among would-be gardeners is buying seeds but never putting them in the ground.

FINDING MORE INFORMATION

Obviously, this isn't a how-to book on gardening. For in-depth gardening information and plans, I suggest you purchase *The Resilient Gardener* by Carol Deppe, *Gardening When It Counts* by Steve Solomon, or *The Sustainable Vegetable Garden* by John Jeavons and Carol Cox.

✔ *Today's Assignment:*

Evaluate your space and needs and then plan a survival garden. Research your region for the best crops and planting times, buy gardening tools, and assemble your seed assortment. Be ready when the time comes to plant the various seeds.

Take a trip to

the gunshop.

What's the perfect survival gun? That question has been asked many, many times over the years, and more than a few survivalists have attempted to answer with their own favorites. But for the most part the effort has been in vain because the real answer is: none exists. Some firearms are indeed more versatile than others, but none is up to the task of doing everything well. Repeat after me: *"There is no perfect survival gun."*

You need a battery of firearms to cover defense, foraging, concealed carry, and other tasks, but you don't have to spend a lot of money. Below I have outlined five arsenals, each covering a broad range of tasks, needs, and budgets. If nothing else, my suggestions should generate discourse.

"I WORK AT WALMART" ARSENAL

- ❑ Mosin-Nagant '91 rifle
- ❑ Single-shot 12-gauge shotgun
- ❑ Smith & Wesson Model 10 revolver

"GOVERNMENT WELFARE" ARSENAL

- ❑ Short Magazine Lee-Enfield (SMLE) rifle
- ❑ Mossberg Maverick 88 12-gauge shotgun
- ❑ Smith & Wesson Model 10 revolver
- ❑ Ruger 10/22 rifle

Above: Most sporting-goods stores stock a good selection of firearms, but you should know what you need before you walk through the door.

Right: A Mossberg 12-gauge pump-action shotgun and a Savage Scout rifle in .308 will suffice for most foraging needs.

"I HAVE A FULL-TIME JOB" ARSENAL

❏ Ruger Mini-14 Ranch Rifle or AR-15
❏ Mossberg 500 12-gauge shotgun
❏ Glock Model 19 pistol
❏ Ruger 10/22 rifle

"TWO JOBS AND MAXED CREDIT CARD" ARSENAL

❏ Ruger Mini-14 Ranch Rifle or AR-15
❏ Remington 870 Express 12-gauge
   shotgun with spare riot barrel
❏ Glock Model 19 pistol
❏ Ruger 10/22 rifle
❏ Winchester Model 70 bolt-action rifle in .308 Win.
❏ Taurus CIA Model 850 .38 SPL revolver

"YUPPIE SURVIVAL" ARSENAL

❏ L1A1 or Springfield Armory M1A rifle
   chambered in .308 Win.
❏ Remington Model 7 bolt-action rifle in .223
❏ Winchester Model 70 bolt-action rifle in 308 Win.
❏ Remington 870 Express 12-gauge shotgun
   with spare riot barrel
❏ Colt 1911 A1 .45 ACP
❏ Taurus CIA Model 850 .38 SPL revolver
❏ Savage Model 24F combo, .223 Remington over
   12-gauge (if you can find one used)
❏ Ruger 10/22 rifle
❏ Barrett 82A1 .50 BMG rifle

It should be noted that these firearms are merely suggestions based on what I've owned and can recommend from personal experience (with the exception of the Barrett 82A1, which I have never owned). These recommendations aren't written in stone, and there are many substitutes you could make without a

If the shooter does his part, .22-caliber pistols and revolvers are excellent for taking small game.

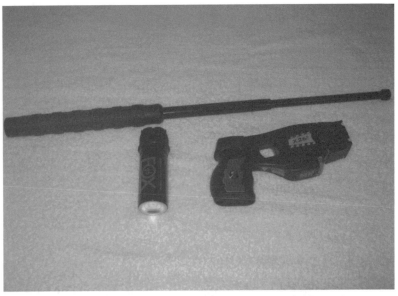

Having the option of nonlethal self-defense is always a good thing: OC spray, Taser, and extendable baton will take care of many personal-defense situations.

loss in quality or versatility. For example, a Smith & Wesson revolver of equal dimensions or even a Glock 26 could replace the Taurus CIA. Or you could switch the Colt 1911 A1 for one made by another company or even a Springfield Armory XD chambered for the .45 ACP.

GUNS *NOT* TO BUY FOR SURVIVAL

Countless books and magazines advise you how to choose the "best" survival gun. What I haven't seen is a list of firearms that should be avoided. I think this is a mistake, because knowing what *not* to buy is just as important as knowing what to buy.

I'm sure many will disagree with my conclusions or have other examples that I've failed to mention. In some cases, it isn't a matter of my overlooking or forgetting to mention a certain manufacturer or firearm, but simply that I have no experience with that particular firearm or manufacturer. I only give advice on things I've personally used, tested, worked on in my shop, and fully evaluated. Here are my thoughts in this area. Take them for what you will . . .

- Phoenix Arms: low price and low quality
- Lorcin: cheaply made, with poor quality parts
- Hi-Point: carbines, fair; handguns, prone to failure
- Bryco: jam, fire, jam, fire, jam, jam, broken firing pin
- FIE: well known for inferior quality; currently out of business
- Llama: some good weapons, others junk—best to avoid the lot
- Sterling: mediocre quality and usually unreliable; currently out of business
- Charco Arms (formerly Charter Arms): chambers rough, action tends to lock up, and exhibit tendency to shave lead
- Intratec Tec-9: low-quality construction, inaccurate, will not reliably feed hollowpoint ammunition
- Norinco: quality control hit and miss; some products seem pretty good considering the price, others not so much

☑ Today's Assignment:

Get a copy of *Boston's Gun Bible* by Boston T. Party and consult it before putting together your survival firearms arsenal. Then head to a dealer to buy firearms based on the recommendations above, in *Boston's Gun Bible*, or from someone you trust who is experienced in all aspects of survival firearms. And don't forget ammo.

Put together a

survival kit for

your automobile.

Most of us spend a lot of time in our cars, so we need a car kit in addition to our every-day carry (EDC) kit. Below are lists of items for two different kits: the deluxe and basic. Choose the one that best fits your needs.

DELUXE KIT

- ❏ Change of clothes, depending on season
- ❏ Duct tape
- ❏ EDC kit (see day 28)
- ❏ Energy bars or similar food
- ❏ Fire extinguisher
- ❏ First aid kit
- ❏ Fix-a-Flat can
- ❏ Flashlight and extra batteries
- ❏ Folding shovel
- ❏ Fuses
- ❏ Hand cleaner, waterless (e.g., GoJo)
- ❏ Hose clamps
- ❏ Ice scraper
- ❏ Jack and lug wrench
- ❏ Jumper cables
- ❏ Light sticks, two
- ❏ Matches

This auto survival kit has gotten me out of many tough spots while on the road.

❏ Motor oil, windshield washer fluid, engine coolant; 1 gallon each
❏ Road flares
❏ Sleeping bag or wool blanket (weight appropriate for season)
❏ Socket set
❏ Spare tire
❏ Special needs items: prescription medications, eyeglasses, hearing aid batteries, and items for infants if applicable (e.g., formula, diapers, bottles, pacifiers)
❏ Tire chains for snowy climates
❏ Tire plug kit
❏ Toilet paper
❏ Tools: flat-head and Phillip's head screwdrivers, pliers, vise grips, and adjustable wrench
❏ Tow chain or rope
❏ Water (drinking), 1 gallon
❏ Whistle
❏ Wire

BASIC KIT

- ❏ Duct tape
- ❏ EDC kit
- ❏ Fire extinguisher
- ❏ First aid kit, small
- ❏ Fix-a-Flat can
- ❏ Folding shovel
- ❏ Hand cleaner, waterless (e.g., GoJo)
- ❏ Jack and lug wrench
- ❏ Jumper cables
- ❏ Spare tire
- ❏ Toilet paper
- ❏ Water (drinking), 1 gallon

✔ *Today's Assignment:*

Put together a car survival kit based on your budget, terrain, and needs.

Brainstorm ideas and

look for gaps in your

preparations.

A simple trick I use to find gaps in my emergency preparedness plan is to ask myself what I would do if I knew TEOTWAWKI was going to start in 31 days. Keeping this in mind, I look at my situation, skills, and supplies, and make a list of ideas using a "mind map." (Wikipedia defines a mind map as a "diagram used to represent words, ideas, tasks, or other items linked to and arranged around a central key word or idea. Mind maps are used to generate, visualize, structure, and classify ideas, and as an aid to studying and organizing information, solving problems, making decisions.")

This trick has helped me find shortcomings that would have gone unnoticed had I not set a deadline for starting my preparations for TEOTWAWKI and mind-mapped ideas. For example, the last time I did this, I found that I needed to learn more about trapping wild game, expanding my use of spices for cooking, and using hydrated lime for waste disposal. I try to do this exercise at least every other month.

When you do this mind-mapping exercise, it is important to have the correct mindset. While it's true that none of us knows the exact start date for TEOTWAWKI (or has it already started?), for this exercise to be most effective you have to do your best to envision it happening on your chosen date. If you don't take the date seriously, you'll fail to see important deficiencies in your plan, thus ensuring that the process is a waste of time.

Once you have the proper mindset, in the middle of a piece of paper write down your start date for TEOTWAWKI. Now brainstorm ideas for what you need (and can) do to prepare for that date. For each gap in your plan, draw a conversation bubble around your TEOTWAWKI date and write down how you intend to fill in the gap. The key at this point is to be creative and think outside the box as much as possible. Any idea is allowed at this point. Don't overthink; just write down the ideas as they enter your mind. The illustration above contains a six-month TEOTWAWKI start time and some sample tasks that might be appropriate for your plan.

Today's Assignment:

Set your TEOTWAWKI date and mind-map what you need to do to increase your preparedness for that date.

Build a deadfall trap with a figure-four trigger.

Those of you who have been following my blog (www.thesurvivalistblog.net) already know that I plan on using trapped and hunted wild game to supplement my stored food, domestic animals, and garden. I don't think having only one food source after the crash is wise, as many things could happen to my primary food storage. My motto is to always have plans C and D to back up plans A and B.

Most trappers consider the figure-four trigger to be a disposable resource to be made, used, and thrown away; however, I prefer to make and use the same trigger multiple times and at different locations as needed. This saves a lot of time and energy when contrasted with having to make a new trigger every time one is needed.

Because of this, I tend to take more time and care when making triggers than most trappers do. I choose only dry, seasoned hardwood pieces that are approximately 1-inch thick so they won't warp or shrink during the natural aging process. I also take great care when cutting out the notches that hold the trap together.

The most crucial element, and the one most often overlooked by beginners, is that all the notched and grooved areas that make up the trigger assembly should be squared, with all bark removed. If this is not done, the trigger will likely fly apart when the drop weight is activated. The weight can be a large

From this photo it is easy to see how the figure-four trigger goes together.

Figure-four trigger and rock deadfall set and ready to go. Note the barrier placed around the back and side. This will help guide the animal into the correct position. You can tie bait to the end of the horizontal bait stick or do as I have done here and partially bury the bait behind the trigger (under the drop weight).

rock, log, or another object heavy enough to kill your intended prey. You don't want to merely injure the critter. If possible, you want its death to be quick, painless, and humane.

Bait should be fastened to the bait stick before setting the trigger under the drop weight. Otherwise, the weight might fall on your arm. Another option is to partially bury the bait in a small jar at the rearmost point under the drop weight. As the animal digs for the bait it will dislodge the trigger and cause the weight to fall, crushing the critter underneath.

✔ Today's Assignment:

Make a figure-four trigger and deadfall trap. (**Note:** Follow all game laws and set this trap where domestic pets cannot get into it.)

DAY

28

Put together your every-day carry (EDC) kit.

Your EDC kit is one of your most important survival tools because it is the kit that you will always have on your person if an unexpected disaster occurs while you are away from your home, office, or vehicle.

Even though an EDC kit is a much abbreviated version of a larger, more comprehensive kit and is not meant to supply all your long-term needs, it will drastically increase your chances of getting back home to your main survival supplies or surviving an immediate threat to your personal survival, such as a criminal assault or a natural or physical disaster.

For example, let's say you have the misfortune of being trapped alive under the rubble after your office building collapses during an earthquake. Because you have your EDC kit, you are able to use your cell phone or whistle to help rescuers find you. Your handgun or OC spray from your EDC kit can be used to ward off a criminal attack, and you can use the multitool or Swiss Army knife to repair a critical item or fabricate an item from scrounged materials should the need arise.

At the end of the day, the gear that matters most is what you have when you need it, and that gear should be in your EDC kit. Its uses and possibilities for saving your life are infinite, and its contents should be carefully selected.

What you include in your EDC kit will depend on your personal needs and individual location, but certain items should be

Among other things, my EDC kit contains a cell phone, flashlight, handgun, lighter, and Swiss Army knife.

included in most kits. These items are what we will consider here. Include these items in your kit if they fit your needs and add other things that are personally essential to you.

Weight is one of the most important considerations when selecting items for your EDC kit. You'll be carrying this kit with you at all times (or you should be). The last thing you want to do is to leave your kit behind on the very day you need it because you thought it was too heavy or bulky to bother with. Keep it light, tight, and ready to go.

SUGGESTED EDC KIT CONTENTS

❏ Antiseptic wipes, large and individually sealed (first aid, health, and repairs)
❏ Bic lighter (starting fires)

- Cash in small bills (general use, paying for emergency services, and bartering)
- Cell phone (communication, emergencies, GPS navigation)
- Flashlight, small, and extra batteries (signaling, emergency light)
- Handgun, OC spray, or Taser (self-defense)
- Multitool or Swiss Army knife (general use, repairs)
- Prescription meds, at least a two-day supply (health)
- Whistle (alerting help)

Once you decide what you need to carry, you'll need to figure out how to carry those items in the most convenient and comfortable way. If you usually carry a purse or backpack, how to carry your kit isn't a problem because you already have a ready-made container. Just organize the contents in the purse or pack so that they are easy to reach by their anticipated order of importance. For example, you want to have your handgun, OC spray, or Taser in an easily accessible inside location or in an outer purse pocket.

A number of purses/packs have a specially designed pocket for secure and discreet handgun carry, and most also have an assortment of outside and inside pockets for other items in your EDC kit. (**Note:** Because of the possibility of having your purse/pack snatched, you may want to carry your defensive weapon separately.)

Men who don't generally carry a backpack or briefcase have a more difficult time of finding a suitable way to carry a kit. If the kit is kept small and light (as it should be), it isn't much of a problem. I carry the bulk of my kit on my belt, with the other items distributed in my pockets and on my key ring.

Several companies sell specially designed vests for concealed handgun carry that have plenty of pockets, and these work great for carrying and distributing the components of an EDC kit. Because of the general design of this type of vest, the weight being carried is evenly distributed, making the kit barely noticeable.

Another option for men is a small fanny pack, such as the

Uncle Mike's Off-Duty and Concealment Nylon Fanny Pack Gunrunner Holster. These are great for carrying EDC contents with a well-designed and easily reached pocket for your self-defense option.

Today's Assignment:

Put together an EDC kit and start carrying it with you whenever you are away from home. (**Note:** Be sure to follow all weapons laws in your area and those areas you travel to or within—it is your duty to know these laws before you purchase or carry the items in question.)

Learn to cook in a Thermos bottle.

I first learned of Thermos cooking while reading Kurt Saxon's *The Survivor* newsletter back in the late 1980s and have been using this thermal cooking method to save propane ever since. I have no way of knowing for sure, but I would estimate a savings of $40 to $50 per year from my doing this.

In a grid-down situation, using less fuel will be a top priority, and cooking with a Thermos (or other insulated vacuum bottle) will help you get the most from the smallest amount of fuel possible. All you'll need is a small-mouth vacuum bottle (I prefer the Stanley vacuum bottle) and a funnel. Let's take a closer look at how to cook this way.

1.   Start by preheating the vacuum bottle. Simply bring enough water to a boil to fill the bottle, screw on the cap, and set the bottle aside while you do the following steps.
2.   Heat the food in a pot on your stove until it is boiling
3.   Pour out the water used to preheat the vacuum bottle.
4.   Using your funnel so you don't waste any, pour the boiling food into your preheated bottle, and let the heat inside finish the cooking.

That's it . . . Simple, isn't it? Here are several tips to make it even more energy efficient.

- Lay the bottle on its side so the food will cook more evenly.
- Wrap the bottle in a blanket to retain more heat.
- I recommend a small-mouth Stanley (formerly Aladdin-Stanley) bottle and not some cheap knockoff. But if you do get another type of bottle, be sure it has stainless steel insulation inside and not glass.
- A gallon plastic bottle (e.g., milk, bleach, vegetable oil) cut in half makes an excellent free funnel. Just make sure it's clean.
- Shake the bottle every few hours so the contents don't coagulate or stick to the sides.

Cooking time depends on what you are cooking, the type of insulated bottle you use, and the amount of preparation you do before adding the food to the bottle. You'll learn by doing. But don't get in any hurry, because your food will not burn or be overcooked.

You're probably wondering what foods you can cook in a Thermos bottle. I cook whole-wheat breakfast cereal, steel-cut whole oats, rice, beans, lentils, and pasta. One of my favorite dishes is rice with chopped vegetables.

THERMAL COOKING WITHOUT A BOTTLE

Thermal cooking can be done without using a vacuum bottle. This method is more convenient when cooking larger amounts of food, such as for beans.

Thermal-Cooked Beans
You need a large pot with a tight-fitting lid, a wool blanket, and a cooler with lid.

1. Sort and presoak beans overnight.
2. Bring the contents to a rolling boil for about 10 minutes, cover the pot with the lid, and quickly remove the pot from the heat and wrap it tightly in the wool blanket. Cover the pot completely because you don't want any heat to escape.

3. Carefully set the wrapped pot of beans into the cooler, filling any remaining space between the cooler and blanket with insulating material (e.g., old newspaper), and place the lid on the cooler. Pinto beans take approximately three hours to cook completely this way. If the beans are not done to your liking, simply reheat, rewrap, and let stand for another hour.

Thermal cooking can be used to cook anything that you normally slow cook. The advantages of thermal cooking are numerous: you get three hours of cooking time for only 10 minutes of fuel; food does not stick or burn if left unattended; water use is minimal because it does not boil away or need to be refilled while cooking. In short, thermal cooking is the most cost-effective and least labor-intensive method I know.

Note: Some of you may have heard about "cooler corn," where you put raw corn on the cob in an insulated picnic-type cooler and then fill the cooler with boiling water. Then a couple hours or so later (it keeps just right for a long time), you have corn on the cob. The problem is that "cooler" plastics are made to take cold, not heat, and they may leach bad plasticizing chemicals into the cooking water at high temperatures. Now, if you have one of the old aluminum-lined Coleman coolers, you're OK to cook this way.

✔ *Today's Assignment:*

Buy a good-quality insulated vacuum bottle and cook something in it. Also try thermal cooking beans or other dish without the thermal bottle.

Find like-minded survivalist friends.

Many readers of my blog (www.thesurvivalistblog.net) have asked me: "Where or how do I find like-minded folks to form a survival group to help man our retreat?" Unfortunately, I know of several survival groups that are no longer together. It's my observation that most groups fail within the first two years due to a lack of funds, the varying level of seriousness among the members, and infighting. People just can't get along, no matter the need, at least not for long. But I'm sure there are exceptions . . . the successful survival groups are the ones you never hear about.

Those groups that make it through the collapse will be those who meld into their surroundings and avoid making themselves targets. Remember, a fight avoided is a fight won. Having a large group in place can eliminate this impromptu blending. I firmly believe that survival groups should be kept as small as possible while allowing for a complementary skill set within the group.

Finding people with complementary skills, compatible beliefs, and common interests who can form a group and work together for the long haul may seem impossible, and in some cases it is. Yet, no man is an island. Finding the right survivalist friends could mean the difference between a long life and a quick demise.

Several readers of my blog have questioned my living alone in the backwoods. What they don't understand is that although

I live alone, I'm not alone. I have friends and family in the area who will help me if I need it. We will pull together and help each other, naturally forming our own survival group without having to plan it.

Take a look at your family members and friends—would they be there for you and each other if a serious survival situation occurs? What are their skills? What do they have to offer? Have they been storing food, water, and other essential supplies? Can they work together?

If the answers to the above questions are negative, then you need to look elsewhere for support. But where do you look? And, perhaps more important, how do you do it without drawing attention to yourself or inviting danger into your retreat? Consider looking into the following:

❏ Churches with similar religious convictions as your own
❏ Hunting clubs
❏ Gun clubs
❏ Garden clubs
❏ First aid and CPR classes
❏ Martial arts schools and self-defense groups

I'm sure you can think of other possibilities, but you get the idea: look for like-minded people with beliefs that are compatible with your own.

Consider starting your own club, as a ruse to attract like-minded people for an initial feeling-out process. Even if you don't find a worthy candidate, you'll at least have gotten off the couch. I know a former U.S. Army Ranger who offered free wilderness survival classes to find potential members for his survival group. The students would spend a weekend out in the woods learning various outdoor survival techniques, while he secretly evaluated each individual to see how he or she would fit into his group.

Often, finding potential survivalist friends is as simple as networking. But, obviously, you don't want to tell everyone you meet about your survival plans. Even those who seem like likely candidates could be the opposite of what you're looking for when you learn more about them.

It's best to start slow, keeping your options open. Act like you are just as unprepared as everyone else but yet concerned about the future and recent disasters. Say that you would like to be better prepared for such an event but you don't know where to start. If people start giving you advice, listen closely. If the advice is sound, you may have hit pay dirt. Informally talking about your fears and concerns may open up the conversation, but you should still be very careful with whom you share your actual plans.

Trust must be earned over time. You don't want to share your secrets with a government snitch or a future looter. And no matter what happens or how much you're offered, *never* do anything illegal if asked to do so. Remember Randy Weaver?

☑ *Today's Assignment:*

Make a list of the skills you want to have represented in your survival group. Then get out there and start evaluating potential friends to see which ones possess those skills.

Learn to tie a knot.

T his is one area where many "end of the world" survival manuals fall short. Most incorporate information on choosing firearms and storing food, but few tell you how to tie a secure knot. This is an important survival skill, and you can learn how to tie a knot by following the instructions below (reprinted from the *U.S. Army Survival Manual*).

TERMINOLOGY

To be able to construct shelters, traps and snares, weapons and tools, and other devices, you should have a basic knowledge of ropes and knots and some of the terminology used with them. The terms are as follows:

Bight.
A simple bend of rope in which the rope does not cross itself.
Dressing the knot.
The orientation of all knot parts so that they are properly aligned, straightened, or bundled. Neglecting this can result in an additional 50 percent reduction in knot strength. This term is sometimes used for setting the knot, which involves tightening all parts of the knot so they bind on one another and make the knot

operational. A loosely tied knot can easily deform under strain and change, becoming a slipknot or, worse, untying.

Fraps.

A means of tightening the lashings by looping the rope perpendicularly around the wraps that holds the spars or sticks together.

Lashings.

A means of using wraps and fraps to tie two or three spars or sticks together to form solid corners or to construct tripods. Lashings begin and end with clove hitches.

Lay.

The lay of the rope is the same as the twist of the rope.

Loop.

A loop is formed by crossing the running end over or under the standing end to form a ring or circle in the rope.

Pigtail.

That part of the running end that is left after tying the knot. It should be no more than 4 inches long to conserve rope and prevent interference.

Running end.

The free or working end of a rope. This is the part of the rope you are actually using to tie the knot.

Standing end.

The static part of rope, or the rest of the rope besides the running end.

Turn.

A loop around an object, such as a post, rail, or ring, with the running end continuing in the opposite direction to the standing end. A round turn continues to circle and exits in the same general direction as the standing end.

Whipping.

Any method of preventing the end of a rope from untwisting or becoming unwound. It is done by wrapping the end tightly with a small cord, tape, or other means. It should be done on both sides of an anticipated cut in a rope before cutting the rope in two. This prevents the rope from immediately untwisting.

Wraps.

Simple wraps of rope around two poles or sticks (square lashing) or three poles or sticks (tripod lashing). Wraps begin and end with clove hitches and get tighter with fraps. All together, they form a lashing.

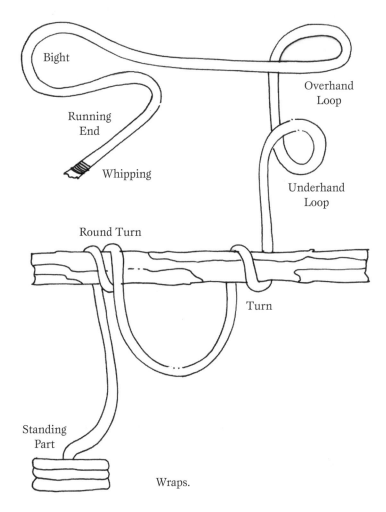

Bight

Overhand Loop

Running End

Whipping

Underhand Loop

Round Turn

Turn

Standing Part

Wraps.

BASIC KNOTS

The 10 basic knots and methods of tying them that you should know for survival purposes are as follows:

1. *Half-hitch.* This is the simplest of all knots, and it used to be the safety, or finishing, knot for all U.S. Army knots. Because it had a tendency to undo itself without load, it has since been replaced by the overhand.
2. *Overhand.* This is the simple knot that most people tie every-day as the first step in tying their shoes. It can also be used to temporarily whip the end of a rope. This knot should replace the half-hitch as a finishing knot for other knots. This knot alone will reduce the strength of a straight rope by 55 percent.

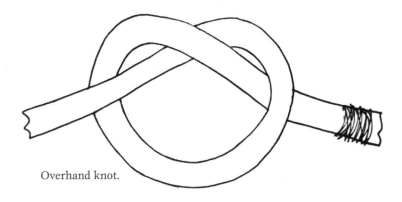

Overhand knot.

3. *Square.* A good, simple knot for general-purpose use, the square knot is basically two overhand knots that are reversed, as in right over left, left over right. It is used to tie the ends of two ropes of equal diameter together (just like your shoe laces) and must be secured with an overhand on both ends. It is easy to inspect, as it forms two loops and is easy to untie after being loaded.

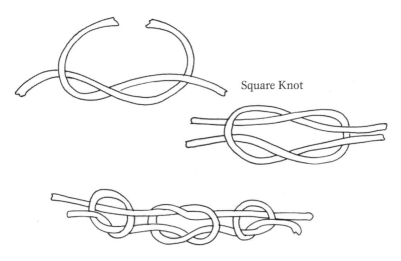

Square Knot

Square knot secured by overhand knots.

4. *Round turn and two half-hitches.* This is the main anchor knot for one-rope bridges and other applications where a good anchor knot is required and high loads would make other knots jam and be difficult to untie. It is used most frequently to anchor rope to a pole or tree.

Round turn and two half-hitches.

5. *Clove hitch and end-of-the-line clove hitch.* These knots can be used to fasten a rope to a tree or pipe, and they put little strain on the rope. They are easy anchor knots, but tension must remain on the knot or they will slip. This can be remedied by making another loop around the object and under the center of the clove hitch.

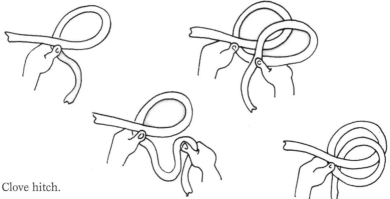

Clove hitch.

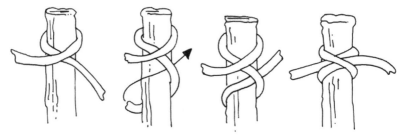

End-of-the-line clove hitch.

6. *Sheep shank.* A method of shortening a rope, a sheep shank may also be used to take the load off a weak spot in the rope. It is a temporary knot unless the eyes are fastened to the standing part of the rope on both ends.

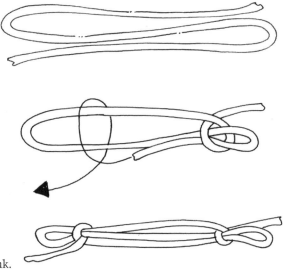

Sheep shank.

7. *Double sheet bend.* This knot is used to tie together the ends of two ropes of equal or unequal diameter. It will also join wet rope and not slip or draw tight under load. It can be used to tie the ends of several ropes to the end of one rope. When a single rope is tied to multiple ropes, the bight is formed with the multiple of ropes.

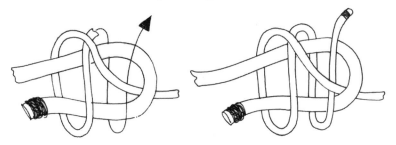

Double sheet bend.

8. *Prusik.* This knot ties a short rope around a longer rope (for example, a sling rope around a climbing rope) in such a manner that the short rope will slide on the climbing rope if no tension is applied and will hold if tension is applied on the short rope. This knot can be tied with an end of rope or bight of rope. When tied with an end of rope, the knot is finished off with a bowline. The nonslip nature of the knot on another rope allows the climbing of ropes with footholds. It can also be used to anchor ropes or the end of a traction splint on a branch or ski pole.

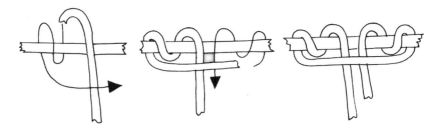

Prusik, end of the line.

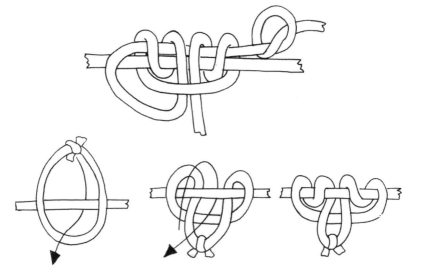

Prusik, end of line, and centerline.

Prusik, end of line with bowline for safety.

9. *Bowline and bowline finished with an overhand knot.* The around-the-body bowline was the basic knot used for rescue for many years, as it provided a loop to place around a body that would not slip or tighten up under strain. It has been replaced by the figure eight in most applications because the latter does not weaken the rope as much.

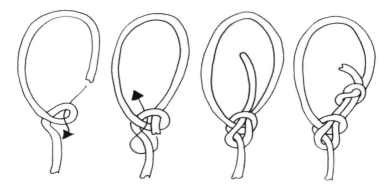

Bowline and bowline finished with overhand knot.

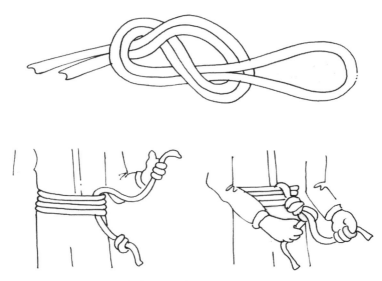

Figure eight and retractable figure eight.

10. *Figure eight and retractable figure eight.* This knot is the main rescue knot in use today. It has the advantages of being stronger than the bowline and easier to tie and check. One disadvantage is that when wet it may be more difficult to untie than the bowline after being stressed. The figure eight (or figure of eight) can be used as an anchor knot on fixed ropes. It can also be used to prevent the end of a rope from slipping through a fastening or loop in another rope when a knot larger than an overhand is needed.

✔ *Today's Assignment:*

Get some rope and teach yourself how to tie the 10 basic knots described above. Check out www.animatedknots.com for step-by-step interactive photos for knot tying. This is a fantastic resource, and there are several other sites devoted to knotcraft that you may want to check out as well.

In your journey to preparedness, I hope that you have learned a lot of things that aren't necessarily quantifiable on a survival checklist. Below are 14 bonus survival lessons, tips, and tricks that I learned along the way on my journey.

1. *You can't do it all at once.* This is a mistake that I and many others have made: we want to get it all done . . . yesterday. You run around frantically determined to become prepared for a major disaster within a week of starting, but all you end up doing is wasting money and time. Relax, make a plan, and work toward your goals steadily but prudently. You'll get there sooner than you think.

2. *You don't have to be rich to have a viable survival plan.* By reading some survival blogs and books, you'd get the impression that you need to spend $100,000 to reach a suitable level of preparedness. Unfortunately, this causes many to give up before they start. You don't have to prep like the rich—you just need to prep smart.

3. *Make your own plan.* No two survival plans should be exactly the same. Granted, there will be some similarities, but each plan must be customized to meet the needs of the individual. For example, I often suggest wheat as the backbone of the survival food storage

plan, but a small percentage of the population is allergic to wheat and will need to store gluten-free foods in equal or greater value. You need to take a long look at your location, skills, and needs, and plan accordingly. Make your own plan.

4. *Preparedness isn't measured by how many guns you have.* I'm sure many of you have made this mistake. When I started prepping, I worried more about finding the perfect survival gun and building an arsenal than completing my other survival preparations. Guns are fun, and it's easy to get lost in their appeal; just don't let other areas suffer while you try to build your dream arsenal.

5. *Skills are more important than gear.* We've all heard the expression, "He who dies with the most toys wins." I'm still trying to figure out what the winning prize is. I have nothing against using the latest technology and gear—just don't depend on it. Things break, get lost or stolen, or don't work as intended. The most important piece of survival gear is your brain. Learning survival skills should be your number-one priority.

6. *You're not Rambo.* Many new survivors fall into what I call the Rambo mindset: they can't wait for the collapse and breakdown of law and order so they can take to the woods and engage in one firefight after another. They see themselves as the ultimate killing machine taking down the bad guys in a burst of gunfire. These "Rambo wannabes" won't last long.

7. *Get a life.* Preparedness is serious business, and it is easy to become obsessed. Don't do it. I love learning new skills, reading survival books, and planning for different possibilities. But these things take a lot of time, and I've learned that, unless I take time off, the rest of my life tends to fall apart. Go see a movie, spend time with family, and relax. Then when you come back to all this, you will do so with a fresh mind, which will allow you to get more done and

make fewer mistakes. The key is maintaining balance between living your life now and preparing for what the future may bring.

8. *Don't just read how to do things.* Most books on survival and self-reliance aren't even read, much less put to use. They are bought, flipped through, and put away—never tested or learned from. This is a mistake. Study the books and attempt top do the activities yourself. This is the only way to learn what actually works.

9. *Have a backup plan.* When I started prepping, I thought all I needed to be prepared was a full pantry. We have all heard the warning, "Don't put all your eggs in the same basket." This is good advice in life as well as in survival planning. Too many things can go wrong—and probably will. You need a backup plan, which brings us to our next point . . .

10. *Remember the number three.* You need to have at least three independent sources to meet all your essential survival needs. Let's take heat for example; you could have a wood stove, propane heater, and cold weather sleeping bags. Power might consist of a backup generator, a small solar setup, and a stockpile of disposable batteries. Food could include an in-home food storage pantry, a home garden, and a secret cache in a secure location away from home.

11. *Include your family.* If possible, get your family onboard so your prepping becomes a family affair. This way, you can learn and spend time together. A family working together toward their preparedness is the best survival group. For example, take a first aid class, hunter safety course, self-defense workshop, or shop course together. Try to make it fun and interesting, and include your family as much as possible.

12. *Diversify your skills.* Diversification ties in with numbers 9 and 10 above and the age-old advice of not putting all your eggs in one basket. Learn as many survival skills as possible. Being a master gardener, for

example, is a great skill that you can make even more valuable by also learning how to preserve and store what you grow. An expert trapper can increase his chances of survival by also learning to forage for edible plants. You get the idea.

13. *Try to do something every week.* By setting a goal of doing at least one thing each week, you will meet your goals earlier and be more efficient in doing so.

14. *Eat what you store.* Most of us have been guilty of this at one time or another—we fill our pantry with unfamiliar foods, thinking we will adapt our diet "when the time comes." This is nonsense. You need to learn to prepare and eat your stored provisions now so they become familiar. This way you weed out waste and any food allergies *before* "the time comes."

DAY ✔ *Final thoughts :*

Why aren't you meeting

your survival goals ?

ongratulations! You have completed your 31-day emergency preparedness survival plan. Give yourself a hand. You've not only learned how to plan for survival food needs, you have assembled a rotating food pantry, planted a garden, and learned how to cook with solar and thermal heat. You've built a water filter and learned other methods of water purification. You've assembled survival kits of various sizes and purposes, as well as your own survival and gardening tools and reference libraries. Plus, you are putting together a group of like-minded people with the survival assets you lack. That's a lot of survival knowledge and actions in just 31 short days.

I hope you actually completed each day and didn't just skip over the days while actually doing nothing. If you fall into the latter group (you know who you are), the information here on meeting your survival goals is for you . . .

WRITTEN VS. STORED

Having your goals written on paper instead of stored in your head means you can refer to that list daily, thus reinforcing those goals and making them easier to do. I carry my list in my pocket and look over it at least once a day. Short-term goals are written on Post-It notes and stuck on my refrigerator door and mirror.

Writing down your survival goals makes them harder to forget. Storing goals in the back of your mind isn't very efficient. Stress and day-to-day life make it easy to become distracted, and eventually you lose sight of those goals altogether. Making a list is the best way to stay on track and get things done. Plus, you get the satisfaction of checking off those goals that you have attained.

Writing your goals on paper makes something happens. They go from imaginary targets to real objectives. They go from dreams to concrete things to do.

A few weeks ago, I wrote down several survival goals of my own. Some, I never thought I would actually meet, but as I took steps to complete them, I saw that they were achievable. Combined with determination and drive, I found that writing my goals down helped turn them into reality.

BIG ENOUGH TO STRETCH

I've set my survival goals high: my main short-term goal is to move to a safer retreat area (or at least one I like better) within the next six months and have a garden started at my new location by the beginning of next growing season.

Those will be challenging, but I figure if I work hard enough, I can do them. And it appears now that I'll meet my goals. I've found land in my chosen area and am working out the details with the property owner.

I'm setting similar fitness and survival skill goals, making them real by writing them down, and then working toward achieving each. My long-term fitness goal is to run two miles with a loaded pack. My skill goals include learning at least one new survival skill per week. That means not just learning by reading, but actually doing when possible.

START NOW

The last piece of advice I have for you is to make your list now. Not tomorrow. Not next week. Not next month. *Now.* If you haven't written out tangible goals, figure out what you would like to do within the next month and the next year. Go ahead—I'll wait. Remember, goals can change. If you realize that a goal on your list is no longer applicable to your situation, cross it out. It is not written in stone. Look over your list and work on these goals daily. By the way, every survival goal you complete builds confidence, empowering you to complete the bigger ones on your list. It's a domino effect.

Now get busy—your survival depends on it.